SPOKEN LOGOS

A 60 Day Journey for the Contemplative Soul

Brett Derrico

Contents

Part 2: Chaos

Introduction

The Spoken Logos Journey is not your traditional devotional. I am not presenting a daily list of spiritual "to do's" or religious hoops to jump through. The language of Christianity is "done", not "do". The devotional is a 60 day-long journey to unlearn a lot of unhealthy views we have been taught about God and ourselves and to rebuild a new foundation on the pure Gospel of Grace as delivered by Jesus. It will challenge you at points of age-old dogma but can lead to an entire paradigm shift as we look at the meaning of original words, certain verses lost in translation, and by shining new light (really old light; it's in line with what the early church and mystics believed) on the bible through the lens of God as Love and Jesus as the Word. My hope is that right believing will lead to right action and a growing awareness of completeness that will transform the reader and world at large. Be prepared to fall deeply in love with your Creator!

This book is written in two parts, Part 1 Order and Part 2 Chaos, for the seeker to both grow more theologically and to adventure ever deeper mystically. Too often it is one extreme or the other. Either one gets stuck in orderly dogma and doctrines which leads to a stale and stagnant orthodoxy with little experience or one gets lost in the chaos of their own subjective experiences while lacking strong theology, therefore never undergoing authentic maturation and transformation. Ultimately having a solid foundation of strong Christology will allow the seeker to boldly embrace mysteries because they are in fellowship with the Mystery. Understanding will open the door to experience, right thought will pave the way for transformation and true embodiment, and good theology will lead to a meaningful mysticism. One will feel confident to approach God with open hands and allow the Mystery to disclose itself to them.

This contemplative reading is an easy-to-understand condensed synthesis of numerous pioneers of Christian thought, both ancient and modern. Profound truths are relay-ed in simple language so as not to be a barrier of esoteric theology but rather to prove accessible for the common reader and even beginners starting on their spiritual quest. However, a good amount of scripture and word translation is provided to serve as a resource for those well versed in biblical knowledge yet sincere about searching for truth. I am indebted to numerous authors whose works I immersed myself in for several years. If I was aware of inspiration from these works, I included them at the end of the chapter. I rely heavily on Francois du Toit's *Mirror Bible Translation* for Greek and Dr. Neil Douglas Klotz for Aramaic. All Bible translations used are indicated unless I paraphrased a verse. The italics and bold lettering throughout the devotional are my own addition to draw attention to certain words or parts of scripture. In some instances, important topics that are touched on earlier in the devotional are further elaborated on later.

Although Spoken Logos can be used as a daily devotional, I highly recommend each chapter be accompanied with referencing the scriptures provided, meditation, and contemplation. If you are led to camp out around a certain truth, stay there as long as necessary. I attempt to include my own experiences only when appropriate as I feel it is essential to allow the Spirit to minister to us in the deepest layers of our own unique personhood.

"If you marry the ordered to the chaos,
you produce the divine child."
Carl Jung

contemplation: a state of mystical awareness of God's being

(*Merriam-Webster*)

Part 1

ORDER

Day 1 | Just Dance

"God is not just a dancer; God is the dance itself."
Richard Rohr

"In the beginning God...". This is one of the most profound statements in the entirety of scripture. Before there ever was heaven and earth or time itself, who was this Creator in the beginning? What we believe about this God speaks volumes concerning what we believe about ourselves and our place in the cosmos. It's easy to imagine an isolated deity up in heaven somewhere who decided to create out of sheer boredom; a distant mover who is consistently let down by his creatures and always frustrated and disapproving with the failings of humanity.

But we find throughout the Bible that this God was never alone, even from time eternal. In the beginning was the Word, face to face with God, and the Spirit hovered over the face of the deep. In the very act of creating, God declared, "let *us* make man in *our* image." Therefore, in the beginning was the inconceivable fellowship and communion of the triune God- the Father, Son, and Holy Spirit. Perceiving this blissful relationship is vitally important to our understanding of each other and all of creation. The early church fathers referred to this as *perichoresis*; the mutual indwelling and communion of persons Father, Son, and Holy Spirit in the One God*; or simply stated the Divine Dance. This is a perfect, other-centered, astonishingly beautiful love dance within the Trinity. The Father is always pleased with the Son saying, "hear him", the Son loves the Father and "only does what the Father does," and the Spirit continually testifies of the Son. There is no "to do" list, shame, or insecurity in this relationship; no striving to please one another or earn each other's approval. Just a love bed of pure ecstatic enjoyment. And from this "divine womb" the cosmos was birthed.

To know that we were made in the *image and likeness* of this Eternal Dance allows us to see who we truly are at the inmost levels of our being. No wonder Jesus told Paul that it is better to give than to receive. This was not mere advice to be a better person. Love is our most authentic self and genuine freedom will be experienced at the moment of awakening to this. Seeing our origin in the face of the Trinity gives us divine insight into our deepest reality; we were created from a selfless, other focused, and relational blueprint. We are meant to dance together and be in the game of life together in other-centered love. Although there may be contradictions at the moment in your life, the unveiling of the truth will cause you to start manifesting this reality. This is where true freedom lies! Believe and you will see!

Incarnation: The Person and Life of Christ by T.F. Torrance

Day 2 | The Divine Exchange

"For the Son of God became man so that we might become God."
St. Athanasius

There is something special about the sixth day. Not only does the Hebrew translation indicate a uniqueness about this day but it is also the first day of creation that God emphatically declares, "it is very good!" Man and woman were God's crowning achievement, His *image signature* on the creative masterpiece of the cosmos. And then on the seventh day He went into His sabbath rest. The seventh day is eternal; there is never any mention of an evening and a morning like all of the other days in the Genesis account. This day stands outside of time.

Time in the first chapter of the Bible is a difficult and extensive topic to cover in a devotional but there are definite parallels between the creation account in Genesis and the incarnation of Jesus Christ. It seems to communicate that this is one seamless creative act or one day; the *sixth day*. In reference to God saying in Genesis 1:26 "let us make man in our image," the word for man is *anthropos*. As Jesus stands trial, after being whipped and scourged by the Roman authorities, Pilate says, "Behold the man!" Behold the *anthropos*! A few hours later, on the *sixth day* of the week, Jesus proclaims, "it is finished." Mankind has been completed in Him.*

Isaiah gives us excellent insight into what took place here. He states in Chapter 52:14 NIV that many were appalled at the appearance of Jesus during his trial. He had been physically "disfigured beyond that of any human being and his form marred beyond human likeness." What's going on here? Jesus was bearing the image of Adam. He became what we are so we could become what He is. We were not made in the image of Adam; we were made in the image of Christ. To be Christ-like is what it means to be true man and true woman. Therefore, Jesus is the first fully human being; the firstborn of many brethren, a new creation, a new race. Although we all experience the fall of the first man Adam, we find our deepest and most substantial reality in the face of the new man Jesus.

Now we live on the edge of the sixth day. In the incarnation of Christ, the eternal has intersected with the temporal. The seventh day has invaded the sixth day. And according to Hebrews, we are invited into God's eternal seventh day rest in the here and now. What does it mean to enter God's rest? It says in Zephaniah that "He *rests in His love* and spins around in delight and jubilant joy at the thought of you!" (Mirror) God's rest is His celebration of you, His child. A celebration of completeness, perfection, and love. To rest is to see yourself the way God sees you; through the creative act of His Son in which we are made righteous, perfect, and sanctified. When we entwine our thoughts with God we rise up on high with wings like eagles, above contradiction, and experience eternal rest!**

The History of Time by Peter Hiett
**God Believes in You* by Francois Du Toit

Day 3 | A God Made In Our Image

"It's a scary thing to realize that while the Lord made us in his own image, we have been creating him in our own ever since."
C. Baxter Kruger

I believe we all have memory of Eden deep within us. A longing for the innocence and bliss Adam and Eve experienced in the garden of pleasure. There is something extraordinarily desirable when we envision the carefree life before the fall. Theologian Baxter Kruger refers to this as the "baptism of assurance."* Adam and Eve knew who they were and they knew whose they were. They walked in secure intimacy with their Creator in the cool of the day, naked and unashamed.

We often associate the partaking of the fruit as the Fall but this was not the case. The Fall took place when their assurance was lost. This occurred in their minds first and then the fruit of that was...well...eating fruit. Assurance was lost when they started to believe lies about God and themselves. "Did God really say that? Is He withholding something from me? Is He good after all? Maybe I need to do something to become more like Him?"
From this point forward, they would be defined by performance

instead of beings who were already like God, made in His divine image.

Instead of running into God's embrace Adam and Eve hid in the bushes, naked and ashamed and blaming each other and God as they feared the judgment and wrath of an angry deity. They had never seen any of these characteristics in God before so why were they seeing them now? God never changed; they did. As they wrestled with guilt and shame over their actions they started to project angry streaks across the face of God. In other words, they created a god made in their own image. All the way up until today, most people still believe in this type of god. If we feel like a failure then we see God as disappointed. If we have self-hatred then we see God as disapproving. If we are prejudiced towards others then we see God as retributive.

Where are you Adam? Probably the most detrimental lie we believe when we see God this way is that He is distant from us. It seems easier to imagine God as far off when we perceive ourselves as failures. But it is *us* who withdraws from Him. It says in Isaiah 59:2 NKJV that "your iniquities have separated *you* from your God." It doesn't say God separated from us. We are the ones that pull away and hide. Paul explains this as being alienated and setting up God as an enemy in *our own minds*

(Colossians 1:21). God knew where Adam was. There was no distance from God's perspective. The only separation that exists between us and God is *the thought* that we are separated from God.

How do we get back to Eden? Didn't God put a flaming sword that "turned every way" to block us from entering? The Hebrew word for turned is *haphak* meaning to turn about, to change, *to be converted*, to turn back, to return.** Repent, or metanoia, means to know together with God. The Sword always *pointed back* to mankind's original identity; it pointed back to paradise.

Jesus and the Undoing of Adam by C. Baxter Kruger
** *The Mirror Study Bible* by Francois Du Toit

Day 4 | Scripture is the Manger

"It is Christ Himself, not the Bible, who is the true word of God."

C.S. Lewis

The bible is not the Word. It is clear in the very first verse of the gospel of John that Jesus is the Word; the Word from the beginning who was both *with* God and *was* God. Although the scriptures are inspired, they should be used to point to the Author. God's ultimate intention was not that the Word would end in a lifeless book that we would follow like a behavior manual. God is about incarnation; the Word made flesh in both the advent of Christ and in our own lives.

When Jesus (or any writer of the New Testament) referred to the Scriptures, he was talking about the Old Testament. And he always referred to the Scriptures as *pointing to himself.* "You search the Scriptures, for in them you think you have eternal life; and these are they which *testify of Me*" (John 5:39 NKJV). The gospel of Luke tells the story of two companions traveling on the road to Emmaus after the crucifixion. They are visited by the resurrected Jesus who discloses to them in the Scriptures, from the beginning of Moses to the Prophets, all things concerning *himself.* When their eyes were later opened to see Jesus at the breaking of bread, they said to one another, "didn't our hearts burn within us while He opened the Scriptures to us" (Luke 24:32). This is when we know we have moved from dead religion to something living; when we see the Jesus everywhere in the bible and our hearts burn ablaze with revelation and understanding.

When we believe Jesus is the Word, we start seeing Him all throughout the Old Testament. Indeed, the Word was on a long journey from eternal beginning to be made flesh in the incarnation of Christ. This is called typology. There are countless examples of typology in the Old Testament but one of the most profound doctrines that is hidden in the Scriptures is the "one for the many" doctrine. Just three of the multiple instances of this belief finally fulfilled in Jesus as the ultimate "one for all" are the stories of Adam, Noah, and Abraham; there was something quite profound being ingrained in the minds of the people of God.

Paul makes it clear that Jesus is the last Adam; the *eschaton* Adam, the ultimate Adam. The main correlation that Paul is making between the two is the representative capacity that they both functioned in. We had nothing to do with Adam's sin but nevertheless, sin and death impacted *all* men. How much more, did the life and work of Christ, the Lord from Heaven, give righteousness to *all* men? Peter makes a correlation between Noah's flood and baptism. Just as the entire earth was baptized except 8 survivors (8 symbolizes regeneration, resurrection, new order, rebirth), the entire cosmos both then and now was baptized in the death and resurrection of Jesus. And the Scripture "preached the gospel to Abraham beforehand, saying, "In you *all* the nations shall be blessed" (Galatians 3:8 NKJV). By one man's faith *all* are blessed. There is one Lord, one faith, one baptism; the one of Jesus that has included us all through grace. The one for the many. One for all.

Day 5 | Who's the Old Testament God?

"He who has seen me has seen the Father."
John 14:9 NKJV

How many people can honestly say they are fully sure that God is good? Of course Jesus is good, full of grace and mercy, willing to forgive and save. But it almost feels like He is hiding an angry Father behind his back; a Father who had to kill his Son to be able to stomach us, right? Furthermore, the God of the Old Testament seemingly looks nothing like Jesus and it's almost inconceivable to reconcile the two. Didn't the author of Hebrews also say that Jesus (God) was the same yesterday, today, and forever? How can we possibly harmonize Jesus with a God who wanted Abraham to kill his son Isaac, commanded Israel to slaughter tribes in Canaan, and who introduced a law code with punishments similar to Hammurabi?

We need to recognize that throughout the Old Testament *humanity* is the one who is evolving their understanding of God and not God who is constantly changing. God is good. He was good yesterday, He's good today, and He will be good tomorrow. In fact He is so good that He meets us where we are at and not where we should be. And this is exactly where He found Abraham, the man who is considered the founder of the Hebrew people. Abraham was from Ur of Mesopotamia. It was common to sacrifice their firstborn to appease the thousands of deities they worshiped. God met Abraham exactly where He was at; in the darkness of his paganism about to perform an unspeakable act to His son Isaac. And He turned the light on in that darkness. "I am not like the gods of your ancestors Abraham. I provide the sacrifice. Look behind you in the bushes to see the lamb slain from time immemorial."

From this event on Mount Moriah, it was a slow process of the Lord leading Israel by the hand out of their paganism and incorrect beliefs about who their Maker was. God would have preferred intimacy with His people. The Abrahamic covenant was one of grace. But the people were not ready to go there yet. They felt too insignificant to be near to God so they asked for law to put distance between themselves and Jehovah. And God, again meeting the Israelites in their darkness, met them where they were at and provided a way for them to draw close to Him. Even still, the entire law was based on types and shadows pointing to Jesus. God was preparing furniture in the minds of His people so that they would have understanding when Christ suffered his passion. By the time of the Prophets God began to introduce a new way of mercy and not sacrifice. "Sacrifice and offering *You did not desire*, But a body You have prepared for Me" (Hebrews 10:5 NKJV).

There are even more concrete examples showing this human evolution of thought. In Numbers 16:41-49 it reads that *God was responsible* for consuming thousands of Israelites with a plague for complaining. But when Paul shares this story in the New Testament (I Cor.10:10) he says *the destroyer* was responsible for the plague. In II Samuel 24, God apparently moved *David* to take a census and then punished David after he obeyed. But hundreds of years later in I Chronicles 21, with much more God experience under their belt, *satan* is implicated as the culprit for moving David to take the census*. If you've seen Jesus you've seen the Father. Now read the Old Testament with this lens.

A More Christlike God by Brad Jersak

Day 6 | The Vicarious Man

"From beginning to end what Jesus Christ has done for you He has done not only as God but as man. He has acted in your place in the whole range of your life and human activity."
T.F. Torrance.

Most Christians understand that there was a God-to-humanward movement when the Son came to us in human form. They believe that Jesus the messiah came to do something *for* them. But after coming to hear the work of Christ, everything else gets thrown back on the believer to make this a reality. It becomes about their own faith, their own repentance, their own dying and rising etc. But this is not exactly good news. The delectable news of the Gospel of Grace is that Jesus fulfilled the *human-to-Godward* movement as well. In other words, He did not just come to do something for humanity; He came to do something *as humanity*. Jesus is the perfect human response to the Father given in our place. Whatever our faith, our repentance, or our decision, it is only a response to the perfect response already made *on our behalf* by Jesus in complete fidelity to the Father.

There are several scriptural references that show this to be true. It says in Hebrews that we should consider the *Apostle* (sent from God) and *High Priest* (represents humanity to God) of our confession. It says in Hosea 6:2 NKJV, "After two days He will *revive us*; On the third day He will *raise us* up, That we may live in His sight." There are numerous examples of Paul saying that we were co-crucified, co-buried, co-raised, and co-ascended with Christ. Even the title "Son of Man" is used to identify the representative capacity that Jesus served on behalf of mankind.

Some believe that the whole "co" teaching is something that happens to them transactionally at the point they believe. Some see the fulfillment of Jeremiah only taking place when they *transactionally* receive a new heart at the point of personal conversion. But we must see the entire vicarious life of Jesus as a redeeming event. Every moment that Jesus was a human being, he was beating back the sinful man and condemning sin in the flesh. He was tempted in all ways like we are yet without sin. We often think that Jesus was some type of super-human that could never identify with our human weaknesses. But Jesus spent his entire life thoroughly converting our fallen humanity and violently cleansing the human temple in his servant body.

There is a reason there is so much talk by the apostles concerning the *obedience* of Christ. Jesus' perfect obedient life at every turn and temptation was thoroughly *eradicating* the old man. His servant offering to God in our humanity was stitching God's commandments deep within our fleshly hearts. If Jesus was without sin, why do you think he was baptized by John for the remission of sins? "Let it be for now that we may fulfill *all* righteousness." Matt.3:14. He was repenting *for us* and *as us*. By one man's obedience the many were made righteous. Awake O sleeper to the truth of who you are!

Day 7 | The Chosen One

"The doctrine of election is the sum of the Gospel...He is both the electing God and elected man in One."
Karl Barth

If we look through the lens of grace in the Old Testament, we notice that remnants or individual people were never chosen in *exclusion* from everyone; they were chosen to *include* more. Israel was called to be a royal priesthood *to the world*. Their destiny of being a *light to the gentiles* was ultimately fulfilled in the One true Israelite, Jesus. Just like Israel, Jesus was called out of Egypt as a child. Also similar to Joshua and Israel passing through the Jordan into the promised land, Jesus passed through the river Jordan in baptism. And as Israel was in the wilderness for *forty* years, Jesus was tempted by the devil in the wilderness for *forty* days. Jesus is the fulfillment of the "one for all" type in the Old Testament. He is the chosen One.

We did not choose God. And to be technical, God did not choose us. We were chosen *in Christ*. This (in Christ, in Him) is Paul's favorite phrase used in his writings over 153 times. This phrase correctly understood is the key to understanding Paul's writings and will begin to unlock unfathomable dimensions of grace when we see it. We are crucified *in Him*, baptized *in Him*, seated in heavenly places *in Him*, righteous *in Him*, elect *in Him* etc. Jesus is God's chosen one for all humanity. If you read Ephesians chapter 1, God's plan from the very beginning was "to gather together all things in Christ." Throughout the whole chapter, it talks about His will, His grace, His good pleasure, His purpose etc. It is God's doing that we are *in Christ;* it was a complete act of grace performed by God to us.

Romans 9-11 deals with the topic of election and is one of the more confusing portions of scripture to make sense out of. Unfortunately this has been to the detriment of the character of God. Since Paul's letters were spoken by him orally as someone recorded them, he often takes *a long time* to make his point (such as Rom.9-11). So there is a key scripture that we can look at first to see where Paul is going with this.

Ending in Chapter 11:32 NKJV, we see Paul's conclusion; "God has committed them *all* to disobedience, that He might have mercy on *all.*" Try to imagine a big sifting (like an hourglass) going on in the Old Testament through chosen people and remnants all the way down to the Chosen One Jesus. So all seeming "exclusion" in the Old Testament ultimately leads to the most *inclusive* act in Christ for all humanity.

Now, we go back to 9 to see one of the main themes that Paul is addressing; the unfairness of grace! "I will have mercy on whomever I will have mercy, and I will have compassion on whomever I will have compassion" (Exodus 33:19, Romans 9:15 NKJV). Paul's main argument is toward his Jewish audience addressing inclusion of the gentiles. He is using diatribe, a sarcastic discourse, showing all of the times that grace was working unfairly in their favor! "Remember when it seemed like God flipped the power structure on its head, and chose Israel over Pharoah? Or when God chose Jacob the younger over the firstborn Esau ignoring hereditary rules? Well now He is doing the same thing for the gentiles too in letting them in on your blessings." The grace of God is unfair. He is pure goodness to all!

Jesus is the elected one for all. We've been blessed with every spiritual blessing in Him!

*This chapter was heavily influenced by *Chosen for Paradise: The Inclusion of Humanity in the Saving Act of Christ* by John Crowder

Day 8 | Christology 101

"Salvation is the very person of Christ Himself. The essence of his very being is incarnation- oneness between Heaven and earth. He mediates not as a mere action but simply by being God and humanity in the same package".
John Crowder

The first three gospels are known as the Synoptic Gospels (Matthew, Mark, and Luke). In these accounts we see Jesus mostly making statements like, "I show you the way, come follow me. I speak the truth, hear me. I will give you life." Much later on we have the arrival of the most mystical of the four gospels, John. In this account Jesus boldly proclaims, "I AM the way, the truth, and the life." It truly is inspiring that a lot of people are coming into the finished work these days. But Paul said, I have determined to know nothing among you except Christ **and** him crucified. He is showing that we cannot separate the *Person of Christ* from his finished work. The early patristic fathers spent centuries fighting heresies and hammering out this important idea of who Jesus is.

Jesus is fully God and fully man. He doesn't teach us ways or give us examples of how we get into union with God. As the God-man, **he is** our union with God. Many historic icons often depict Jesus bringing two fingers together, revealing this union. In Christ, heaven and earth have united. Temporal and eternal have intersected. God and man are one. Jesus said, "on that day you will *realize* that I am in My Father, and you are in Me, and I am in you" (John 14:20 NIV). He didn't say that you would need to do something to climb into God. He said you would one day *awaken* to this truth.

We have been lifted up into communion with the triune God, but that is not just in this life. Our union with God is an eternal relationship anchored in the person of Christ. The incarnation is not just a 33-year-blip that ended when Jesus died. The bodily ascension has proven this to be an ongoing reality that will continue forever. At this moment there is a flesh and blood human being seated at the right hand of God. And we are there also, seated with him in heavenly places.

For too long we have looked at the many blessings of God as "somethings" that Jesus doles out to the worthy. "Here is some salvation! Here is a little justification for you! How about some righteousness? Here, have some sanctification!" Whenever such things are viewed through this lens, distance is implied which leads to us having to do something to condition God into supplying these gifts. But all of the above mentioned things are a Person; Jesus *is* salvation, he *is* justification, he *is* sanctification, he *is* perfection. And we are too; in Him by a sheer act of grace.

In the life of Christ, something happened to us. In reference to our fallen humanity, Gregory Nazianzen said "the unassumed is the unredeemed." Jesus became every bit of what we were so we would become every bit of who he is. He assumed all of our sickness (when he healed people in the gospels he often groaned), sin, and alienation from God and by virtue of his eternal deity, vicariously healed it in his servant body.

I John 2:8 NKJV states, "a new commandment I write to you, what thing is true in him *and in you*, because the darkness is passing away, and the true light is now shining."

What's true of him is **true of you**. You look just like Jesus!

Day 9 | Christology 102

"The gospel is not the news that we can receive Jesus into our lives. The gospel is the news that Jesus has received us into his."
C. Baxter Kruger

So how do we move from a self-generated look at salvation to a Christ-centered perspective? For too long, salvation has been seen as a commodity that we transactionally receive based on our faith, our repentance, and our altar call. But salvation is not a commodity...it is a Person. Salvation is not so much a question about "what" or "how" but about the "Who". When Zaccheus the tax collector started rambling on about all the ways he planned on making right on his past wrongs, Jesus said, "today salvation has come to this house." Since this was before the cross, this was not a transactional award for Zaccheus's stellar repentance. Jesus, Mr. Salvation, was referring to himself. The very name of Jesus means salvation; God with us.

You may ask, "I thought you needed to be born again to enter the kingdom? The word "again" is *anouthen*; it means from above, the very first, from the top of the list. Jesus was telling Nicodemus that you need to perceive an origin that goes back long before your earthly birth to see your eternal beginnings. Paul voices this when sharing his "conversion" experience in Galatians Chapter 1; "when it pleased the Father who *separated me* from my mothers womb to reveal His Son *in me*" (*en emoi*). For Paul's whole life, he had identified with all of his credentials through the tribe of Benjamin, circumcision as a Hebrew etc. But God had *separated* him from this earthly identification and revealed to Him that he had always been in association with Christ.*

The word "adoption" in the Bible is misleading. We look at it as a transaction where we come from outside of the family and are brought into a new family. But this is not the true meaning of the word adoption, *huiothesia*. The meaning is more akin to a jewish bar mitzvah where we were already part of the family and are now being publicly recognized with the full rights of sonship and inheritance.** Think of the prodigal. Although he was off fast living and squandering all of his inheritance, his sonship was never in question. He was a son all along. The Father's house and everything that the Father owned was his. Eventually he returned and claimed what was his by grace. Salvation is not a matter of "if" but a matter of "*when*." When do we grow up as mature sons and daughters?

Jesus is the covenant given to us by God. There is an interesting speech given by Joshua (the Jesus type) when he claims, "as for me and my house, we will serve the Lord." Then he says to Israel a few verses later, "but you cannot serve the Lord" (Joshua 24:15,19 NKJV). Jesus wasn't relying on humanity but rather vicariously served the Father for us and as us and now has opened our eyes to our household inheritance. This was done on our behalf *before* we had anything to say about it; "while we were powerless, sinners, and enemies" (in our own minds). And what of our repentance, faith, altar call? etc. These should be seen as *firstfruits* of salvation, not prerequisites.

Salvation is not a mere transaction. As covered in previous days, It is our recreation and an enduring relationship that has been forged completely within the person of Jesus Christ!

* *The Mirror Study Bible* by Francois Du Toit
** *The Cosmos Reborn* by John Crowder

Day 10 | Old or New?

"The law was our tutor to bring us to Christ."
Galatians 3:24 NKJV

I remember when I was new to the faith, I would hear others talk about how much they loved the Sermon on the Mount. I would never vocalize it back then but I was terrified by it! Those red letters on the pages of my bible seemed so condemning that I couldn't understand how people could find joy in reading it. Where was the grace in having to follow a narrow path that few could find? How was I supposed to be perfect even as my Father in heaven was perfect. And if you even look at a woman!

This may come as a shocker to some but the Gospels are not really New Testament books, despite being placed there in our bibles. It says in Hebrews 9:17 NKJV that "a testament is in force *after men are dead,* since it has no power at all while the testator lives." So the New Testament does not go into effect until the very end of the gospel accounts when Jesus dies. That would mean the majority of these books are taking place under the Old Covenant. That is why Jesus made a comment about the least in the kingdom being *greater* than John the Baptist. John was the last major prophet operating under an old system which was about to fade away with the arrival of the new.

So how do we make sense out of some really harsh and confusing teachings from the mouth of Jesus? In case you hadn't noticed, Jesus was not a grace teacher! In fact, he actually taught much stricter law than Moses had. "You have been told that you should not murder *but I say* to you if you are angry with someone you have already committed murder in your heart" (Matthew 5:21-22). He was actually taking the law of Moses and making it even more difficult to fulfill!

Jesus did teach grace but in a very hidden way that was actually pointing to Himself. He would teach about the "narrow gate and difficult way" that few could find, only to reveal later, "I AM the gate! I AM the way!" What we must understand is that Jesus is attempting to thoroughly frustrate the religionists of his day; those who felt that they could earn salvation by obeying outward regulations of the law. But the law according to Paul was not meant to obey; it was meant to expose our failure and futility in self-reliance to try and get right with God. It was the schoolmaster to lead us to Christ. Jesus spent a good portion of his ministry teaching hyper-law to try and get people to give up on their self-efforts and turn their attention to him, the Messiah. Jesus didn't always *teach* about grace because He *is* grace!

The law was given so that sin would increase. But where sin increased grace abounded much more! Jesus is the fulfillment of the law for us and in us. When you start reading the word through the lens of the Word you start seeing silver linings of grace everywhere. Law is no longer our teacher. "For the *grace* of God that brings salvation has appeared to all men, *teaching us…*"(Titus 2:11 NKJV). Grace is our teacher now!

Day 11 | The Kingdom is Within

*"God cannot be found "out there" until God
is first found "in here," within ourselves."*
Richard Rohr

It is common among Christians to believe that they need to do something to "get" the kingdom or that something needs to happen before the kingdom comes. But the interesting fact in the parables concerning the kingdom is that the very thing sown **is** the kingdom. It is already here. In the parable of the leaven, the leaven was mixed in the measure *from the very beginning*. And this is the mystery; there has never been a moment that this world has been kingdomless.

From the beginning of creation, the kingdom had been latent in the earth but was made evident in the incarnation. It now has a face. Jesus said that the kingdom was *at hand*; a current and ever present reality. Yes, the mystery that was hidden from ages and generations had now been made manifest. What is this mystery? Christ in you, the hope of glory.

The kingdom isn't just a mere power or influence like the force in Star Wars. It is the very Christ image on the inside of every human being. Jesus said not to look out in the heavens for the kingdom; he said it is *within you*. And do you know who he was talking to when he said that? A hated pharisee. Every human being bears the divine image, the *imago dei*, whether they know it or not and Jesus came to point to it and call it out. When asked by the Pharisees whether it was lawful to pay taxes to Caesar, Jesus displayed a coin and asked whose image it was. In response to the identification of the image of Caesar, Jesus replied, "render to Caesar what is Caesar's. But you, who bear the image of God; render to God what is God's."

Jesus, in reference to the founding of the church, said to Peter, "I have given you the keys to the kingdom." For too long, the church has been using the keys to attempt to get the kingdom "into people", acting like they are the janitors of salvation. But if the kingdom is already within everyone, the keys of the church act to unlock the kingdom from *within*! It is the church's responsibility to point to the priceless treasure within every human being and *unlock* it so that the Christ-life finds expression in that individual's life.

All of humanity comes from one Father; we all bear the divine image. It is up to us to see the value in each other and call it to the surface. The very fact that someone is "lost" points out their belonging to someone in the first place. A lost person never loses their value. If I were to lose a dime under my couch, it wouldn't matter how dusty and dirty it got or how long it remained lost. It would still be worth ten cents. People never lose their value to the Father regardless of where they come from or what they've been through. And this is the way we need to see each other as well.

According to the parables, the kingdom will continue to grow. We can participate by determining what the kingdom is, where it is located, and how to unlock it; by seeing others through the eyes of the Crucified.

Day 12 | Which Jesus Do You Want?

"Only good where evil was, is evil dead."
George MacDonald

Whenever thinking of kingdom parables it is evident when all are taken together there are two vital realities present: the kingdom is universal in both time and space and the mystery of the kingdom has always been hidden and encrypted since the foundation of the earth. But the story of the wheat and weeds adds a whole new dimension to how the kingdom functions, even in the presence of evil.

In the story, the farmer sows seed in the field and then goes to sleep. The work has been completed, the good seed has been sown, and now the farmer is trusting the seeds will thrive and grow on their own. But while he was asleep "his enemy came and sowed weeds among the wheat." When the wheat eventually started to grow, the weeds were present with it. Upon seeing this, the farmer's workers asked if he had indeed sowed good seed in the field and where the weeds came from.

This is the question that everyone asks: where does evil come from? If God is good and has created all things good, why is there evil in the world? Because of the omnipotence of God, people often blame Him for the evil that exists. But it is clear that God has an "enemy" who is responsible for sowing the weeds and for evil in this world. The workers want to immediately uproot the weeds and get rid of them. The farmer's answer is the main point to the parable.

"No...when pulling the weeds you may uproot the wheat with them" (Matthew 13:29 NIV). What Jesus is saying is that when we right-handedly assert power forcefully to deal with the presence of what we perceive as evil, it ends up doing more harm than good. Isn't this the unfortunate history of the Church with inquisitions, wars, and conquest in the name of the cross? And isn't this what the Church still does today by different means such as demanding the forced policies of their political party of choice, "just" invasions, and church culture imposed on others? It has been proven that often good intentions become the very evil that it is trying to uproot. It's interesting that the kind of weed mentioned in the parable looks an awful lot like wheat. Although evil is evident in the world, it is a counterfeit; it is the absence of light and truth. Even original goodness that has been sadly neglected, abused, and manipulated at some point.

"Let them both grow together." This is the unpopular answer Jesus gives on how the kingdom operates. The word let (suffer or permit in other translations) is *aphete* which is conjugated from *aphienai*. Numerous times (47 exactly) *aphienai* is used in the context of letting be by forgiveness, such as Jesus on the Cross. "Forgive", *aphes*, is the last thing that He says to His enemies rather than threatening them. The love of God is cruciform and the ultimate expression of the power of forgiveness. The seemingly impossible and in some cases detestable method that Jesus teaches in dealing with injustice is to forgive. He is quite certain that the mystery of the kingdom will flourish and bear fruit even in the midst of the mystery of iniquity.

Now you may be asking, what about judgment? It's funny that this is only two-thirds of the last verse in the parable but we have fixated on the end game for evil as the primary meaning. But the disciples did the same thing by asking Jesus to explain an already straightforward parable and it seems like he was willing to entertain them with the judgment they were looking for. But one last point: after explaining the parable Jesus says, "whoever has ears, let them hear." The explanation of the wheat and weeds is sandwiched between the mustard seed and yeast parables and the hidden treasure, pearl, and net parables. These are much more focused on the universality and efficacy of the kingdom. And eventually, as we will see later, even judgment will be reinterpreted through the lens of the cross.

It's interesting that when Pilate wanted to release a prisoner to the people, he brought out Jesus the cruciform messiah and Jesus Barabbas the right handed insurrectionist. What type of Jesus do people often look to today in order to achieve their personal or political agendas?

*For the three parable chapters I rely heavily on *Kingdom, Grace, Judgment: Paradox, Outrage, and Vindication in the Parables of Jesus* by Robert Farrar Capon. I highly recommend this book for interpreting the parables. It is also essential when reading the parables to see they are not the same thing as moral lessons but a "deliberately subversive paradox aimed at turning our usual mind upside down." -Cynthia Bourgeault, *The Wisdom Jesus— Transforming Heart and Mind—a New Perspective on Christ and His Message (Shambhala Publications, 2008), 27.*

Day 13 | Arms Wide Open

"God is the prodigal who squanders himself."
Karl Rahner

We all are familiar with the iconic parable of the prodigal son. For centuries, the focus of this story has been on the wayward son; how he squanders his entire inheritance and then finally "comes to himself" and decides to return home to his father's house. The parable has become a lesson on the prodigal's repentance and a side-note on the older son's lack thereof. But is this really what the heart of the parable communicates? It is important to remember that the Prodigal Son is a title that Bible translators coined, and not Jesus. A more appropriate title would be "The Father's Wreckless Love." We will see why as we revisit this story in a new light.

It is important to see from the start of the parable that a death takes place. Both sons demanded their inheritance from the Father, to which the Father consented, essentially showing a willingness to prepare a death beforehand* (the lamb was slain before the foundations of the earth). We know what happens immediately after. The wayward son goes off squandering his inheritance on riotous living and ends up laboring in the mire of a pig pen. And this is usually where ministers teach the honor of repentance as the prodigal comes to himself and decides to return home. But a closer look does not show much repentance at all on the son's part: Luke 15:17 NIV reads, "How many of my father's hired servants have food to spare, and *here I am starving to death*!" Did you catch that? The son doesn't feel sorry at all for how he dishonored his father; his immediate concern is his empty belly!**

Then the son starts planning his return, preparing a speech for how he has sinned against his father and is no longer worthy to be a son but will become *a hired servant* in his house. And don't so many of us do the same thing when we first come to God? We try to approach Him not as a good Father, but on the basis of *transaction* where he has to be conditioned to bless us or answer our prayers. But when the son was "a long way off" the father had compassion and ran to him and embraced him (before the son repents!). The son starts regurgitating his planned speech but the Father cuts him off before there's even a mention of hired servitude.** "Get the robe and ring! Prepare the fatted calf! For this son of mine was lost and is found!" (Lk.15:24)

You see, the prodigal's sonship was never in question from the

Father's perspective. Even when lost he was always a son. If you are looking for repentance, this is where I believe the son actually shows "*metanoia*", or sees things the way his father does. He realizes that servanthood is never going to fly in his good Father's house so he just receives his lavish grace and goes to the party!

What of the older son who is bitter towards his father for the scandalous grace his undeserving brother has just received? "My son...everything I have is yours." See, we all are sons and daughters of the Father with an unimaginable inheritance. These two sons are representative of all humanity who have access to this unspeakable gift whether we know it or not. Do we go inside to the party or do we remain outside toiling in the world? Even if we are stubborn about joining, like the older son, the good Father stands *outside* continually beckoning us to enjoy what is ours by grace!**

Kingdom, Grace, Judgment: Paradox, Outrage, and Vindication in the Parables of Jesus by Robert Farrar Capon
**The Cosmos Reborn* by John Crowder

Day 14 | Christ the G.O.A.T.

"Hell has no choice but to be within the power of the final party, even though it refuses to act as if it is at the party. It lies not so much outside the festivities as it is sequestered within them. It is hidden, if you will, in the spear wound in Christ's side to keep it from being a wet blanket on the heavenly proceedings." Robert Capon

For the judgment parable, we will look at one of the most evocative of all parables; the Great Judgment and the dividing of the sheep and the goats. Most people feel like this is the most cut and dry. "Finally we will hear about the judgment that we have been so anxiously waiting for!" Eternal separation and punishment for the wicked and peace and joy forever in the Lord's presence for all of the good. Admittedly this is one of the more fiery of the parables but there might be a reason for that, and several silver linings of grace if we have eyes to see!

It is essential to understand the ministry of Jesus on this side of the cross. As we said before, His earthly ministry in the gospel accounts was almost entirely directed towards the super spiritual religionists of the day. Jesus spent a lot of time confronting and frustrating law followers who were still trusting in their own self-righteousness to achieve holiness and salvation. His teachings were meant to press on people to force them to give up on self-effort and striving as a means of producing life and to see Himself as the life-giver. With the parables, we see the judgment ones getting more and more "hot" as the day of judgment, the crisis, was soon approaching.

Several people interpret this parable to be about Jesus separating Jews rejecting the faith from Gentiles but that doesn't make much sense. For one, Paul sums up his long discourse in Romans chapter 11 by saying all Israel will be saved. Secondly, all of the church before Paul was a Jewish believing body. Jesus is simply saying that "all the nations will be gathered before Him." "All Nations" was referring to non-Jews; this was actually showing the inclusion of the gentiles along with the nation of Israel! Remember, parables were intended to entirely subvert a prior way of thinking and including the gentiles would definitely have that effect. When the son of man was lifted up, he drew *all* to Himself!

But what about the separating? Although there is a dividing of the sheep and goats, notice that it is all done *within* the shepherding of the Great Shepard. Shepherds tended both sheep and goats. The sheep might be God's but so are the goats.

All this is showing is how serious God is about the party! He will not let the goats bring their self-pity and poor attitudes to put a damper on the celebration. They may be goats but they are His goats!

Why the separation then? We often take a dualistic approach to the parables between the good and the bad, the moral and the immoral, those who believe and those who don't. But the people who inherit the kingdom in this parable don't seem to necessarily fit this criteria. They don't really know what they did or when they ever saw the Lord! It seems like they are just willing to put dumb blind trust in the open invitation instead of in their perfect works and faith. They simply accept their acceptance! An interesting point is that often people who believe they are serving God and are fixated on heaven and hell do the least for "the least" in this world while those not consumed by the afterlife often are involved with the pressing issues on the earth.

Now wait a minute! What about eternal punishment? The Greek translation of this phrase is *aeon kolasis*. We think of eternal as meaning endless time, such as year after year after year etc. forever. But *aeon* has two meanings, neither of which relate to our concept of eternity. It can mean an era or age with a beginning and end or intensity of time* (such as sitting in a class you dislike for 5 minutes but it feels like 5 years!). And *kolasis* is a horticultural word for pruning so more fruit can come forth. So taken together, eternal punishment could mean a time of pruning or intense experience of correction.

Kingdom, Grace, Judgment: Paradox, Outrage, and Vindication in the Parables of Jesus by Robert Farrar Capon
Love Wins by Robb Bell

Day 15 | Judgment Day

*"Jesus does not save us from the judgment of God-
Jesus IS the judgment of God, to save."*
Peter Hiett

In the modern western world, we have much different definitions of justice and judgment than how they saw these terms in biblical times. Justice to us means retribution or "an eye for an eye" but is this biblical justice? God through Zachariah (7:9 NIV) had this to say about it; "Administer *true justice*; show *mercy and compassion* to one another". Judgment to us is more along the lines of punishment and Roman jurisprudence but the Greek word is *krisos*, which means moment of crisis or truth. If this is the case, what is the judgment of God concerning us?

It says in John 5:22 NKJV "the Father judges no one but has committed all judgment to the Son." A few verses later Jesus follows up with, "I did not come to judge the world but to save the world." When these two verses are put together it becomes clear that Jesus did not come to judge us. So how do we make sense of the judgment of God and when does it take place?

An often quoted verse is John 12:32 NKJV, "And I, if I am lifted up from the earth, will draw all peoples to Myself." Although "all peoples" were drawn to God in reconciliation with the crucifixion of Christ (God was in Christ reconciling *the cosmos* to himself), it just says *all* in the earliest manuscripts. We actually have to go back a few verses earlier to see what Jesus is referring to when he says "all." "*Now* is the judgment of this world; *now* the ruler of this world will be cast out" (John 12:31 NKJV). So when Christ was lifted up, he was drawing *all judgment* to himself. So was Jesus saving us from the judgment of an angry God?

We still look at the term atonement in a pagan sense; as if God was angry at us and needed to see the blood of his Son in order to forgive us. But atonement is easier understood if we think of it as at-one-ment: God making us *one* with himself. God is not the one whose mind needed to be changed; it was our minds! We were the ones who were still running from our Father and hiding from him, thinking we could draw near only through pagan blood rituals. We were the ones who had set up God as the enemy. The cross wasn't to change God, it was to change us! The blood was for us! Hebrews 10:22 NKJV states, "let us draw near with a true heart in full assurance of faith, having *our hearts sprinkled* from an evil conscience."

The cross is the revelation of the heart of the Father towards us. When He showed up in human form, we spit in his face and crucified Him. In return he acted in mercy and compassion by forgiving us and even using our rebellion to forever bind us to himself in eternal union! We gave him our worst and he gave us his best. The Cross is a concrete demonstration of the love of God and *judgment* toward us.

Referring to this appointed day when the Son of God *judged* the world, Acts 17:31 NKJV says "He will judge the world *in righteousness* by the Man whom He has ordained." Through the finished work of His Son, God judges us as righteous! Our innocence has been redeemed! Jesus is God's Eternal Word spoken over you; He is God's mind made up about you!

Day 16 | A Familiar Tune

"He has not despised nor abhorred the affliction of the afflicted; nor has He hidden His face from Him; But when He cried to Him, He heard." Psalm 22:24 NKJV

"My God My God, why have you forsaken me?" We have heard this teaching numerous times. This is the moment that Christ is bearing the sin of humanity on the cross. The Father, who is too holy to look upon sin, has to turn his face and abandon His son. In this moment of darkness, Jesus is forced to experience alienation from God because he is paying the ultimate price for our disobedience. The trinity seems to be falling apart right before our eyes.

I believe this doctrine of penal substitution has created an uncertainty in the deep conscience of people's minds. Although they may give lip service to God being love, faithful, and a good Father, there lies in their psyche a fear about being abandoned when they need Him most. We think, "If scripture confirms that God forsook Jesus, then he quite conceivably could forsake me!"

Psalm 22 is known as being one of the most detailed prophetic chapters of the sufferings of the Messiah on the cross. But because of the lens we have been taught to see through, the first verse about Jesus being abandoned is often taken in isolation from the rest of the chapter. The Psalm that starts off with suffering actually turns into one of *praise and deliverance*! Because it was Messianic high times and rumblings of the coming savior would have been prevalent, everyone would have been familiar with Psalm 22. By Jesus quoting the beginning of this chapter, all of the spectators would have immediately had the whole psalm playing in their minds; and seeing the line for line fulfillment of each verse!

They would have seen the mocking and shaking of heads, tempting God to come to his aid. As the song was playing in their minds they would have witnessed the piercing of the hands and feet of Jesus, the dividing of His garments, and the casting of lots for His clothing. As they watched this unfold they would have begun to see, and some say, "truly this was the Son of God!" But did they also witness Jesus being forsaken by God?

You see, Jesus was stepping into our blindness and asking the question we ask when we experience suffering and injustice. "Where are you God? Why are you allowing this to happen to me?" But He was entering our darkness to turn it into light, and our words of blame into a song of praise and trust in God. He was vicariously bearing our alienation and feelings of abandonment from God and opening our eyes to the Father's love!

Jesus was never forsaken by God. God was *in Christ* reconciling the world to Himself. He said before the cross in John, "I and the Father are One...all of you will forsake me but I will not be alone because *my Father is with me.*" By the time we get to the middle of Psalm 22, Jesus begins praising and declaring His trust for God, "You have answered me...He has not despised nor abhorred the affliction of the afflicted; *nor has He hidden His face from Him*; But when He cried to Him, He heard." Up until his last breath, Jesus demonstrated unbridled trust and fidelity to His Father. "Father, into your hands I commit my spirit." And then Psalm 22 TPT ends with, "and they will all declare, it is finished!". The Father never abandoned his Son and He will never abandon us!

* The majority of the above Psalm 22 discourse comes from *The Cosmos Reborn* by John Crowder

Day 17 | High Priest Y'all!

"Jesus comes from the Father to be the true priest, bone of our bone, flesh of our flesh, in solidarity with humanity, all races, all colors, bearing upon his divine-human heart the names, the needs, the sorrows, the injustices of all nations."
James B. Torrance

When understood aright, the High Priesthood of Christ can bring incredible peace to our walk. We all know that Jesus fulfilled the *righteous requirements* of the law, which was more of a behavioral fulfillment of the law. Most of us can understand grace this far but then it often gets thrown back on us to respond appropriately to Christ's work. This can often lead to condemnation if we don't *feel* secure in our acts of worship before God. But the book of Hebrews focuses on how Jesus also fulfilled the *ordinances of worship* for us and in us!

The first thing that is important to see is that the incarnation of Christ was not limited to his earthly ministry in which Jesus fulfilled his mission and then disappeared in a puff of smoke. It is an eternal reality that continues up until today. Jesus is seated at the right hand of God and "ever lives to make intercession for us" (Hebrews 7:25). He continues as our high priest in the Holy of Holies praying for us, believing for us, and worshiping for us.

We have to go to the Old Testament to correctly see how the Priesthood functions. It is here that we notice a double movement on the part of the high priest; *from man to God* and from God to man. On the day of Atonement, while the rest of Israel stood outside the temple praying, the High Priest would enter the Holy of Holies alone. On their chest they wore a breastplate that had all of the names of the tribes of Israel inscribed on it. So the High Priest, the one for the many, would sum up all of the prayers, worship, and repentance of Israel by his offering in the temple. And when the rituals were done, the Priest would return with the Blessing of Aaron, "May the Lord bless you and keep you. May he make his face shine upon you" (Num.6:25).*

Jesus, the apostle (representing God to man) and High Priest (representing man to God), also fulfilled and continues to fulfill this double movement. With all of humanity stitched into his heart he responds to God perfectly on our behalf. This is what it means to pray in "His name." It's not just a formula that we attach to the end of a prayer to give it more punch. Through the Spirit, we are invited into *His* perfect communion with the

Father to pray through *His* perfect faith, *His* purity etc.

Worship is not just something we do. It is a gift of grace. Just as God *provided* Israel with a way to respond to Him in covenant worship, so has he already provided for us the *one* perfect response and sacrifice of His Son Jesus. We now participate in the perfect worship from the Son. We can boldly bring our feeble faith, our inarticulate words when we don't know what to pray, and our doubts into the Holy of Holies with Jesus, and our High Priest sanctifies it perfectly and prays for us.* We can rest in the One who does have perfect faith on our behalf and who continues to worship perfectly for us. This makes worship much more fluid as we rest and allow Jesus to worship through us!

Worship, Community, and the Triune God of Grace by James B. Torrance

Day 18 | "I Confess!"

"If Jesus Christ is God's Word to man,
then Jesus Christ is man's word to God."
T.F. Torrance

Historically, confession has not been known as something fun we do in the spiritual walk. It has become an act of self focused drudgery in which we engage in endless navel gazing and bringing to our minds all of the mistakes we've made in days/weeks past. We constantly keep short accounts for our behavior and live in a perpetual state of sin-consciousness. But is this what God is asking us to do? Is this what confession really is?

The Greek word for confession is actually a combination of two words, *homo logeo*. It means to speak the same thing. In context of when it is used in John, to speak the same thing as God.* It means to see ourselves the way God does and agree with His view. So what is God speaking that we should confess? There is no more condemnation for us! We are the righteousness of God in Christ Jesus! We have been forgiven and made accepted in the Beloved! Our old sinful nature has been co-crucified with Christ etc. So confession doesn't actually lower us to beat ourselves up and think less of ourselves. It actually raises us up to a higher level of understanding pertaining to our identity and true self in Christ Jesus!

My favorite story showing this in the Bible is when the resurrected Jesus is sitting around the charcoal fire eating with Peter and the other disciples. The word for charcoal here is *anthraka*. Another place where charcoal (*anthrakia*) is mentioned is in Isaiah chapter 6:5 NKJV in which the prophet confesses, "woe is me, for I am undone because I am a man of unclean lips." Right after Isaiah's confession, a seraphim grabs a glowing coal with tongs and places it on his mouth.

In times past, we have been taught that God is actually agreeing with Isaiah's confession and is purging him from uncleanness. But did you ever stop and think that God is actually purging Isaiah's confession? That He is disagreeing with Isaiah's view of himself and is cleansing his inferior confession and putting a new confession in his mouth? Because if you look at a few verses later, it's almost like God is saying, "let's run that back Isaiah and try that one more time. Whom shall I send? Who will go for us?" to which Isaiah responds, "Here I am! Send me!". How does God respond? "Now we are talking, son! Now we are speaking the same thing! Go, and speak to the people!"

So let's go back to the story of Jesus and Peter, chatting around the fire. The last time Peter stood around a fire he had made a confession about his Lord, denying him; "I do not know him. I do not know him! God damn it, I do not know him!" And then heartbroken, he wept bitterly. But now Jesus is bringing Peter back to that same memory to redeem it and put a new confession on Peter's tongue; "I love you Lord. I love you Lord. You know I love you Lord!" Now he is confessing and speaking the same thing as God!

Confession should actually be a very uplifting, and dare I say fun, activity before God. So let's speak the same thing as God; we have been made perfect, sanctified, and righteous by His Son. The next time you confess, do not tell God about your sins; tell your sins about your God!

The Mirror Study Bible by Francois Du Toit

Day 19 | Orphan Eyes

"If you believe a lie long enough it will become truth to you."
Jack Frost

Several years ago, it was a struggle for me to go to church. At the time, I was going through a really challenging period of my life dealing with loss, financial issues, and many other things. Instead of feeling better by going to church, other's joy, dancing, and victorious testimonies were painful to witness. God felt so distant to me that I began to believe in deism (thus an end to bible reading and talking with God). It seemed like anything that elders, pastors, or even my wife tried to encourage me with would only be shot down with my pessimism and negativity. The situation seemed hopeless and I could not see any light at the end of the tunnel. A stronghold had developed in my mind that could not be penetrated.

It wasn't until I was confronted, in plain writing, with the concept of orphan thinking that my healing began to take place. I saw a chart which compared 20 ways of how an orphan sees compared to how a son or daughter of God sees and I was in the orphan column for every single topic.* At that moment, I was completely exposed. All of the anger, bitterness, and hurt that I was carrying for my whole life overwhelmed me and I could do nothing else except sob uncontrollably. I was an orphan.

There are uncountable ways that can lead one to develop orphan thinking. It can range from extreme trauma in childhood to one lie or experience that a person holds on to in their psyche. Whatever the case, the orphan spirit develops a lens through which one views themselves and the world around them. In other words, it begins to dominate their thinking and creates a false view and reality of life. *Everything* ends up being filtered through the orphan lens until it develops into a stronghold of stinking thinking.

When a person has a strong prescription of orphan lenses, their view of God and the sense of processing the Christian life becomes distorted. God is perceived as a task master rather than a loving Father. The orphan will always strive for blessing, status, and inheritance instead of living from the bountiful inheritance that their good Father has already given them. God always feels distant and disengaged rather than intimate and close. If an orphan hears a message about the

63

love of the Father, they will immediately perceive that they need to condition God into loving them through good behavior and other disciplines. If they hear of the goodness of God via the testimonies of others, the orphan only hears, "that will never happen to you."

So what can be done about this? The most important thing initially is the awareness of it. It is also vital to understand that this is a stronghold. A stronghold often cannot simply be *cast out* by a prayer. It needs to be replaced by a *new* stronghold of love, light, and truth. Perfect love casts out fear. The light annihilates darkness and the truth destroys lies. So to start, replacing orphan thoughts with those of a son or daughter is helpful. But ultimately the pure Gospel of grace and the finished work of Christ is what brings life to death and despair. Christ crucified is the power and wisdom of God!

*From Spiritual Slavery to Spiritual Sonship by Jack Frost

Day 20 | Will God Deny Me?

"If we are faithless, He remains faithful."
II Tim. 2:13 NKJV

Will God ever deny us? You have read the scripture before and it says in IITim2:12 NKJV, "if we deny him, he also will deny us." One may start to worry about the possibility of denying God, like Peter once did. "What if I tell somebody I don't know Jesus? How can I make sure that I will never deny him in the future, even if my life depends on it? Or maybe I have already denied him?" Do we deny Jesus when we don't read and pray enough or when we willfully sin?

This portion of scripture (IITim.2:11-13 NKJV) seems to be graceful initially and then this statement is sandwiched smack in the middle of it. Are we reading this correctly? The answer is no, so we will comb through the verses as I give commentary on each one. "This is a faithful saying…". So we are about to hear a faithful statement, a full-of-faith statement. "For if we died with him…". It is important to see that most "if" statements by Paul are not conditions, they are conclusions. They usually come after a "therefore" or in this case a "for." So Paul is concluding, as he mentions in several other verses, that because we have all died with Jesus, we have also been raised with him and therefore live in the power of his resurrection!

"If we endure, we shall also reign with him." Again, this is a conclusion. It says in Romans that we are more than conquerors through Him and will reign in this life. "If we deny him, he also will deny us. If we are faithless, He remains faithful. He cannot deny Himself." The word for deny is *arneomai* which is actually better translated as *to contradict*.* So what this part of the verse is saying is that if we contradict God and what he believes about us, He's going to contradict us right back! This is actually one of the most graceful verses in the New Testament!

Even when we remain faithless about ourselves and how we view our shortcomings, God remains faithful! He is full of faith about you! By His estimate, He is fully persuaded of what His Son accomplished on the Cross. He actually believes in the finished work and our righteousness and holiness before Him. God who has spoken a word over us, the Word, is absolute truth and so cannot contradict Himself. He knows the truth about us and is full of faith about who we are!

Sometimes our actions or behaviors can seem to be a

contradiction of who we are as sanctified, righteous, perfect sons and daughters of the most High. It is easy to get down on ourselves and begin to lose faith in these moments. But when we remain faithless, God is faithful! When we contradict our true nature then He will continue to contradict us right back with His faith and truth about us.

I love seeing this in Peter, whose original name was Simon. Simon means *reed*, which is blown to and fro by the wind. This marked the disciple, who would one second get revelation from God and in the same conversation get revelation from Satan. In one moment, he was defending Jesus from soldiers in Gethsemane only to deny him minutes later before a little girl. But Jesus *contradicted* Simon. "That's not who you are Simon Barjona. You are a Rock. Your name is Peter the rock and your confession will be the foundation stone of the church. And one day, you will refuse to deny me, even in the face of execution. You are a rock brother!" So let God "deny" you over and over. He knows the truth of who you are and believes in you always!

The Mirror Study Bible by Francois Du Toit

Day 21 | Whose Faith is it Anyway?

"The life which I now live in the flesh
I live by the faith of the Son of God."
Galatians 2:20 KJV

Have you ever asked yourself whether you had enough faith to believe in something you were hoping for, sometimes even mid prayer? You become analytical and as faith leaks out, you get even more discouraged knowing that your prayer won't be answered because you are unable to believe. "I wish I had more faith!"

It is interesting that when Jesus was asked by his disciples what they needed to do to perform the works of God, Jesus did not tell them to have faith in *their* faith. He actually took the focus off them completely and said "This is the work of God, that you believe *in Him* whom He sent" (John 6:29 NKJV). In effect Jesus is saying, "believe in me. Rest in the One who does have perfect faith to believe for you. Live by the faith of the Son of God!"

The verse that has so often been quoted, "the just shall live by faith" seemingly throws faith completely back on us. But the correct reading of the text is, "the just shall live *by His faith* or *faithfulness.*" We are supposed to live by His faith! Paul confirms this in Galatians in a few different places. In chapter 2:20, although most translations read as if Paul lives by faith *in* the Son of God, he is actually saying that he lives by the faith *of* the Son of God! Paul didn't live by his own faith or have faith in his faith. He lived by the One who had faith *for* him!

Jesus is Mr. Faith, who has believed and continues to believe perfectly on our behalf. This is the argument that Paul is making in Galatians chapter 3. Although it has been taught that we should live by our faith instead of our works, Paul is not putting one against the other. He's actually saying you shouldn't live by your works *or* your faith. He is saying we should live through His faith! Just like Abraham, whose faith benefited all the nations of the earth, so the faith of Christ the high priest functions on behalf of all humanity!

I am not saying that our faith is not important. Living in a state of anxiety and panic is not our lot as children of God. But Our faith in itself is not something secure to live by. Jesus is the author and finisher of our faith, the conclusion of our faith. Our faith is more the flavor of rest and trust in Him, the One who has perfect faith on our behalf. This allows us to face life circumstances in a state of peace knowing that Jesus knows exactly how to pray and believe for us and hits the mark every time! This is actually what it means when the Spirit intercedes for us. The Greek word is *entunchango,* which means to throw like a javelin; to hit the bullseye!*

When Jesus told his disciples that if they had the faith of a mustard seed they could move mountains, he was not telling them that they had to try and whip up faith within themselves. He is actually telling them they didn't have any faith! He was saying faith as tiny as a mustard seed could move mountains but they didn't even have that! This should not discourage us at all but encourage us to stop striving and simply rest in the faith *of* Jesus!

*_The Mirror Study Bible_ by Francois Du Toit

Day 22 | From Glory to Glory

*"You can't grow in completeness. You can only
grow in awareness of your completeness."*
Francois du Toit

There has been a common teaching in several Christian streams concerning II Corinthians 3:18 about how we keep growing from glory to glory to glory etc. Such teaching gives the impression of not having arrived yet, but we are continuing to grow in newer and higher levels of glory in our walk. If we had an encounter of some sort or if we have a successful platform then we must be at a really high level of glory but if we are not "experiencing" God or have not read and prayed in a while then we are at a lower glory level. This misinterpretation of the scripture unfortunately creates a binary effect where some boast higher levels of glory than others.

So what does *from glory to glory* actually mean? The Greek translation of this portion of the scripture is *apo doxeis en doxan*; this means we have *moved away* from one glory to *arrive and conclude* at another glory. In reference to the whole chapter, it's comparing the Old and New covenants; we have moved away from the Old Covenant to arrive and conclude at something far better in the New Covenant!* So right now we are in the glory! We have already arrived!

Seeing Christ in us, is the hope of glory! Jesus exemplified this convincingly to Peter, James, and John when he took them up to Mount Tabor and transfigured before their eyes. In three gospel accounts, Jesus mentioned that there were some of his disciples who would not taste death until they saw the kingdom come in power! As mentioned earlier, the kingdom is within us and Jesus wanted to clearly demonstrate this to his friends. As He shone like the sun and his clothes became white as light, he was literally "peeling" back his flesh and turning himself "inside out" so they could visibly witness the kingdom and glory!

Peter's only response was to suggest building temples for Elijah, Moses, and Jesus. But while he was mid sentence, God interrupted Him and said, "this is my beloved Son, hear him! Look at what Jesus is showing you! The glory of the old testament and temple is fading away. We are moving to a completely new covenant which is far greater! The human body is now where the glory dwells and is not an inferior temple!"** All of humanity are glory carriers!

You might ask, "doesn't it say in Habakkuk that one day the glory of the Lord will cover all the earth like the waters of the sea?" It actually doesn't say that. It says, "one day *the knowledge of the glory of the Lord will cover all the earth...*". The glory is already here and meant to be unveiled in us. We aren't growing in glory, we are growing in awareness of the glory we carry! One day, people are going to wake up to the unspeakable gift of Christ in them and *this knowledge* is going to flood the earth!

Can you imagine what would happen if we started seeing ourselves and each other as God-carriers? Sounds like heaven on earth! The glory is already here waiting to be revealed. You are glory-full!

The Mirror Study Bible by Francois Du Toit
**God Believes in You* by Francois Du Toit

Day 23 | Let Me Be

"Christianity is a peculiar business! If at the outset we try to do anything, we get nothing; if we seek to attain something, we miss everything. For Christianity begins not with a big DO, but with a big DONE." Watchman Nee

Now that I look back, it's funny how illogical the delivery of the gospel to unbelievers can be. In the same sentence that we tell them what good news we have, we also tell them how lost, doomed, and depraved they are. If that isn't enough, we make salvation dependent on their unbelieving faith and repentance. If someone is halfway intelligent, they must be thinking, "so my depraved faith is the very chain that holds this salvation deal together? What's the point?"

Because we have viewed salvation as some type of commodity that we get transactionally from God, we have looked at our faith, repentance, and confession as prerequisites for salvation. But these are not prerequisites; they are first fruits of salvation. The gospel was never supposed to demand faith from people, it was supposed to supply faith. It says in Romans 10:17 that *"faith comes by hearing,* and that the Word of Christ." To hear that

74

Christ has repented for you and believed on your behalf causes something to spring up on the inside of us. The yoke of bondage gets broken and people get set free. We realize that we are starting at the finish line!

The Christian life is one of continual receiving. Mary, the mother of Jesus, is a type of how the Gospel of Christ should be reacted to. She is told that the son of God has been conceived *inside* of her and she simply replies, "let it be." For too long, we have tried to attain blessing which is really just New Testament law. But really we are told to repent...because the kingdom is *here*! It's the goodness of God that leads us to repentance! Just as Peter repented after receiving a boatload of fish, so we change our way of thinking about ourselves and the Lord when we simply just receive his goodness; when we drink deeply of his love. "We love him because he first loved us." I John 1:19

We often read the bible through a lens of "do in order to become." The behavioral exhortations can be seen as something we need to do in order to get holy or sanctified etc. This bottom up approach mainly crept into the Western Church through Augustine and has been this way ever since. But the Way taught by Paul was "because you are, do." His top down approach is known as the indicative imperative. In every one of

Paul's letters, he spends multiple chapters telling us who we are. "You have been crucified and raised with Christ. You are the righteousness of God in Christ. Don't you know that you are a temple and the Holy Spirit lives in you?" These are indicative statements. Then come the behavioral imperative scriptures; "Husbands love your wives. Honor each other etc." This is who you are, therefore be!

Notice that Jesus never said, *become* holy, *become* perfect, *become* reconciled. He said "*be*." These are benedictions more than things we have to try and become. Jesus has fulfilled the law in us and stitched these things into the very fabric of who we are through his vicarious obedient life. We simply need to receive the truth about us and say, "let me be."

Day 24 | Man in the Mirror

"Christ comes to reawaken us to our true nature. He is our epiphany. He comes to show us the face of God. He comes to show us also our face, the true face of the human soul."
John Scotus Eriugena in Christ of the Celts

A mirror simply reflects the truth about us. There is no judgment, criticism, or condemnation, just a simple reflection of the true self. In IICorinthians 3:18, it reads, "We all, with unveiled face, beholding *as in a mirror* the glory of the Lord, are being transformed into the same image." The implications of this verse are astounding. Jesus didn't come as an example *for* us. He came as an example *as* us!

Jesus came to show us our true face. When we gaze into the face of Jesus, we come face to face with our origin, the blueprint image that we were made in. In Jesus is the Light of life, the light that enlightens everything coming into the world. We are not a faulty design made in the image of Adam, who only served as a type (*tupos*). We were made in the image of Christ. For too long we have treated Jesus as an example for which we need to try and attain holiness through striving and works. But Jesus is our awakening to what is truest about us in the deepest levels of our being.

It says in John 1:12, "as many as received (*lambano*) Him, he gave (*didomi*) power (*exousia*) to become sons of God." Because this reads more like a transaction in most translations, I prefer the Mirror version (the Greek words above are more appropriately translated in the Mirror); "as many as *identified* with Him, He *returned* their *I-am-ness* so they could become children of God."* You see, Jesus was returning something to us that had been ours all along. We all come from one Father and bear His divine image. We had become alienated and forgot the Rock we had been cut from. Jesus came to restore our image and is the revelation of our inheritance as sons and daughters of God.

This is why ontology is so important to our faith and unfortunately one of the least heard teachings in the Church. Ontology is the study of being; in a human sense, what is truest about our nature. Most humans in and out of the Church have been taught that they are born wicked, plagued by the failures of Adam with original sin. When we start seeing such behaviors manifesting, it seems to only reinforce this belief. But Jesus as the last Adam came to eradicate the sinful man on the Cross and rebirth the original blueprint purpose of our design. Ontologically, we have an immortal diamond of beingness on the inside of us. Original goodness and innocence is what is most true about us. Although the impact of the fall is still experienced by all humans, the reality of what happened in the incarnation of Christ is far more ontologically substantial concerning us. We are told to *awake to righteousness* first. And then to *sin not*.

It seems bizarre to me that what Jesus instituted in the holy sacraments in order to focus our mirror gaze *on Him*, actually became a focus entirely *on us*. When we are baptized, rather than identifying with the One baptism of Christ from death to life, we make it about our personal decision for Christ. Instead of taking the eucharist to identify with our new creation reality in the body and blood of Christ, we turn it into an inner sin inspection and guilt trip. The sacraments were always meant to take our eyes off ourselves to see our truth in the face of Jesus; as in a mirror!

* *The Mirror Study Bible* by Francois Du Toit

Day 25 | Christ in the Nations

"Christ is all and in all."
Colossians 3:11 NKJV

At this very moment, every person and living thing in this whole wide world is sustained by Christ. There is nothing that has ever come into existence behind the back of God, but everything was made by Him and for Him. He is in all things and by Him all things hold together. There are no outsiders, no one who is not included, no one who is unloved by God. Everything belongs.

It says in Colossians 3:11 NKJV "there is neither Greek nor Jew, circumcised nor uncircumcised, barbarian, Scythian, slave *nor* free, but Christ *is all* and *in all*. Seems straightforward enough. We should be able to stop right here if it wasn't for our tendency to separate and isolate everything and everyone from the whole. This chapter will be heavy on scripture simply to prove how biblically sound inclusion is. A lot has already been woven throughout the book so we will not revisit all bearing the divine image and the kingdom within or Paul's numerous "all" verses on co-crucifixion and co-raising etc.

Before we get to the multiple early church references by Paul, let's begin with a parable of Jesus. The parable of the hidden treasure, buried in the middle of several parables which each have a catholic universal hint, speaks of a man who found a treasure hidden in a field. He proceeds to hide it and, full of joy, sells everything he has to buy the *whole field*. In the incarnation of Christ, he found extreme value in humanity, re-hid the treasure in earthen vessels, and purchased the entire field! In reference to the surrounding parables, we can see that Jesus was the very Word sown into all the earth.

Paul gives us excellent insight into the mystery of his conversion in Galatians 1. As the murderous Saul is on his way to arrest and kill anyone of The Faith he encounters Jesus. "It pleased the Father to reveal His Son **in me** (*en emoi*), that I might preach Him **in the nations** (*en ethnos*)."* The magnitude of this statement is unfortunately lost in most translations. Paul is saying that he realized the very Christ he was persecuting was inside of him! Now the light shined all around to reveal that Christ was also inside of everyone else!

There are more examples in the book of Acts. When Peter has the vision about God having made all things clean, he comes to realize God is referring to the non-believing gentiles. He says to the house of Cornelius, "God has told me to call no man unclean." In chapter 17, when Paul is dialoguing with pagan philosophers on Mars Hill in Athens, he says "in Him we live and move and have our being, even as your own poets have said, we are His offspring." Paul is telling the pagans they are in on this unspeakable gift too!

We have the best news on earth to share to a lost world; that they are included and belong. People are only interested in what they are a part of. The very preaching of the Gospel of Grace will ignite the seed latent in every person and lead to an awakening!

* *The Mirror Study Bible* by Francois Du Toit

Day 26 | Is God's Wrath For You?

"Man's thought is always of the punishment that will come to him if he sins. God's thought is always of the glory man will miss if he sins. God's purpose for redemption is glory, glory, glory." Watchman Nee

Have you ever heard, "God is love; but he is also justice! God is love; but he is also holy!" People who strongly emphasize these sides of God often portray someone more like Janus, the Roman two-faced God . But is this the Triune God of Grace? The very essence of Yahweh is love so all other attributes associated with Him must be extensions of this love, including even wrath!

Often the meaning of words change shape over time depending on contextual and cultural change. This definitely rings true with our view of punishment and wrath. Our concept of punishment is punitive and our idea of wrath is anger, vengeance, and retribution. But this is not at all the correct view of these words in the time of Jesus. The punishment of God is corrective and always with our best interest in mind!

The wrath of God is even more interesting to break down. The

Greek for *wrath* is *orgeia*, which is more an idea of passion or sudden excitement of the mind. God is crazy in love with us, and like any good lover, passionate about protecting us. His wrath is not anger at us with retribution in mind; it is always about restoration. When we make mistakes or walk away from God, His chief concern is to restore us back to fellowship so we can experience sonship again.

A clear example of how the *wrath of God* works is in Romans Chapter 1, in which it reads, "the wrath of God is revealed from Heaven against *all ungodliness and unrighteousness* of men, who *suppress the truth* in unrighteousness." The first thing important to see is that there is a divine truth about everyone, even if they are ignoring or suppressing it. Secondly, notice that the wrath is against the things harming the person (ungodliness), not the person themselves! So once someone continually walks away from God, lives in habitual sin etc., how does the wrath function?

Three times, it mentions God's response; "God *gave them up* to uncleanness...*gave them up* to vile passions...*gave them over* to a debased mind." See, God will not foster things that are false or harmful to us. He loves us too much. What God will eventually do after continual exhortation met by willful disobedience is to turn us over to reap the consequences of our own ways. We often think that bad consequences mean that God is punishing us. But we are not punished *for* our sins; we are punished *by* our sins. The wages of sin are the punishment. God is allowing us to experience the consequences of our poor decisions so we can learn from them, choose to be restored back in relationship, and bear more fruit!

God is a good Father. Even His wrath is for us and not against us.

Day 27 | Warfare to Joy-Fare

"Those who are Christ's have crucified
the flesh with its passions and desires."
Galatians 5:24 NKJV

"There is a war going on inside of you", they said. "This war is between the flesh and the spirit", they said. "It will be a lifelong battle that you will fight to the end", they said. "The bible teaches this in Romans and Galatians," they said.

How many times have you heard of this division of flesh and spirit inside the Christian believer? It leads to a type of schizophrenia where you can't trust any of your own instincts because you have to "discern" whether it is coming from the flesh or the spirit. You always have to be on your toes, fighting the flesh and feeding the spirit and what makes matters worse is it is seemingly backed up by the writings of Paul. Whatever names we refer to as the flesh; the false self, the ego, the old man etc. has been crucified on the cross with Christ.

So let's take a look at some of these challenging scriptures. Galatians 5:17 reads, "the flesh wars against the spirit, and the

spirit against the flesh, and these are *contrary* to one another."
This is the go-to for everyone that believes in this lifelong battle
within. But did you notice what it is actually saying? The flesh
and the spirit are *contrary* or *opposed* to one another. Think of
trying to put two magnets with the same poles together; they
repel each other! This is what this verse is saying, not that there is
a battle going on within! When we walk in the Spirit, we can't
walk in the flesh; the spirit repels the flesh.* And if we look a few
verses later, Paul says, "those who are Christ's have crucified the
flesh with its passions and desires." This is right in line with
Paul's numerous verses that speak on our past tense crucifixion
with Christ.

Now what I am not saying is that you still can't live by the flesh,
ego, or old man. In fact I think there are a lot of "finished work"
people, including myself at times, who slip up and still live from
this false self. But that's exactly what it is; a farce, a non reality, a
shadow. We may need to do some shadow work in these areas
and simply shine the light in the darkness to reveal the true self.
But we are not supposed to identify ourselves with the old man
because it is not who we really are. We are told to "reckon it
dead"; co-crucified to be co-revealed with Christ in the new man!

People also argue according to what Paul say in Romans 7:14

NKJV, "For what I will to do, that I do not practice; but what I hate, that I do." Here is another verse that is used to justify the inner war. But if you look at how the chapter starts Paul says, "I speak to *those who know the law*." You see, this is not Paul's Christian experience he is sharing; it is his law-based life under Judaism. He realized that the more he tried to follow the law of works in the past, the more sin was revealed in him. The same goes for us today. If we set up a belief system of law and works, we will see sin manifest because that's what the law does; causes sin to increase. And when Paul says, "I die daily" in 1Cor.15, he is referring to the literal potential martyrdom that he faced every day while sharing the gospel.

Instead of constant warfare, live by joy-fare in the truth of who you are in Christ!

Mystical Union by John Crowder

Day 28 | Shall We Go On Sinning?

"I am the bread of life."
John 6:48

I never really faced much kick back from sharing my faith with people until I began teaching the undiluted gospel of grace; and this was entirely from people in the church! Ironically, this is where I also encountered most skepticism because I was not teaching the "good news" (meaning I was not excluding people or trying to save them with the fear of hellfire and judgment). Although Jesus was full of grace and truth, I was teaching some other grace; hyper grace. Don't be surprised if you experience this, you are in good company!

Paul had to address this accusation of hyper grace constantly in his epistles. When you start teaching the finished work and unconditional love of God aka the Gospel, there is an immediate charge of encouraging sin. Paul says in Romans 6:1 NIV, "Shall we go on sinning that grace may increase? By no means, God forbid, What a terrible thought!" NO! Paul is always giving us our death certificate for the old man. What the Gospel teaches is the complete and total assumption and eradication of our sinful man in the life, death, and resurrection of Christ.

The reason for the idea of hyper grace is often an incorrect view of our nature. Most people look at grace as something that is saving us from ourselves and therefore opposed to our sinful nature. But the opposite is true; grace actually flows in harmony with the true self. It awakens us to our godly identity which leads to freedom from sin and the power to live a sanctified life. Paul says that "sin *shall not* have dominion over you, for you are not under the law but under *grace.*" When we live by the grace of God, sin loses its power and we begin to flow in righteousness and holiness.

Anyone who interprets the Gospel on either end of the spectrum--that now I can sin to my hearts content or a religious fear that grace encourages people to live in sin-- does not understand the true Gospel. In fact, either end of this spectrum is dangerous which is why Jesus said to beware of both the leaven of Herod (sin) and the leaven of the Pharisees (religion). These work in tandem with each other in a vicious cycle. When we put ourselves under legalism and regulations, the law does what it is supposed to do and reveals sin. Eventually after continual failure, we just give up, throw our arms up in the air, and swing to the leaven of sin. That is, until we re-commit ourselves with higher standards and the cycle continues. But we are encouraged to live from the leaven of Jesus, the bread of Life, and identify with Him as our holiness!

So what if we do sin? It is important to know that everyone's deeds, both good and bad, are done *in* God; they are immediately enveloped in the Light. The difference is those who come to the light and those who remain in darkness. Those who come to the light, *do truth*. They realize that they have an advocate with the Father in Jesus, that there is no condemnation, and are empowered by forgiveness and grace to be true to themselves. But those who do not believe in Jesus, are condemned already; not by Jesus but by themselves!. They are afraid to bring their evil works to the light because of shame, fear, unbelief etc. If only they could've seen that their works were utterly obliterated in uncreated light, they would have *experienced* forgiveness and freedom!

Grace is not saving you from yourself, it is the truth about you. And when you do make a mistake you have permission to fail forward and fall upward!

Day 29 | The End or New Beginning?

"I am the Alpha and the Omega, the Beginning and
the End...who is and who was and who is to come."
Revelation 1:8 NKJV

We all have heard of the Second Coming of Christ or the Apocalypse. The lake of fire and burning sulfur, the pale horseman, and the seven headed dragon. This is the end; the destruction of the earth by the Son of God who is now riding on a war horse instead of a donkey of peace. Great white thrones of judgment and endless torment and burning for most but peace and joy for the lucky few who remained in God's favor. While you would have to write an entire book to go through the entirety of Revelation, we will go through some main concepts that may open our eyes to new truths and leave us more hopeful than depressed about the fate of humanity.

First is the idea of the Second coming of Christ. We often separate this into two different events of Jesus'; his first entry was about love and peace but the second coming is about judgment and hellfire. But in the bible there is only *his coming*, or *parousia*, and this word is only used to describe the incarnation and return. Thus, these two events are brought together into one continuous event.

The *parousia* is the full manifest presence of God, the culmination of the continual budding and flowering of the Lord's presence on the earth. There is no "new" and "different" Jesus who is now returning to open a can of whoop ass on the human race. Jesus Christ is the same yesterday, today, and forever; full of grace and truth. When John first encountered Jesus in the Revelation, He saw "one *like the Son of man*"; the same Jesus he knew and remembered yet now visibly glorified.

The Revelation of Jesus Christ, is the unveiling or full disclosure of the finished work of Christ. The Cross sent ripple effects into the past and future and is reaching its full manifestation in the *parousia* of Jesus. The Aramaic view of apocalypse was not hyperfocused on the end like we are but on new beginnings. When Jesus physically returns, he is not destroying the cosmos but because of His already finished work, the cosmos will completely transcend into the New Heaven and New Earth.

It is very challenging to decode all of the imagery and timing of something as enigmatic as the book of Revelation. But it seems like a lot of scripture that speak of "the end" such as Matthew 24 and Revelation itself are referring to the actual time of Jesus and the destruction of Jerusalem and the Jewish Temple by the Romans in AD 70 (I personally am a partial preterist; I think most has already been fulfilled but more is yet to manifest). And how about the crazy imagery of the book? It is not anything new and often appears in the Old Testament books, such as the plagues of Egypt and prophetic books. But what is different is that now the *slain lamb* is woven throughout the imagery giving new context to the apocalypse.

Lastly, Revelation is much more graceful and inclusive than you may think. Seven times (7 is an extremely important number meaning completion) there is a reference to all of the different tribes, tongues, and nations coming to the Lord for healing.* And the book ends with an open invitation: "And the Spirit and the bride say, Come. And let him that heareth say, Come. And let him that is athirst come. And whosoever will, let him take the water of life freely" (Revelation 22:17 KJV).

* *The Mirror Study Bible* by Francois Du Toit

Day 30 | What the Hell?

*"God Himself is paradise and punishment for man, since each
tastes God's energies according to the condition of his soul."*
Gregory Nazianzen

What in the hell is hell? We know the common view of endless
eternal burning in a fiery inferno of torment with weeping and
gnashing of teeth. Devils and pitchforks, darkness and separation
from God, with continual punishment forever and ever. Is this
really the fate for most of humanity? While a few perfect peaches
float around in careless bliss in heaven, their family and friends
are being tortured in that "other" place; and they are joyful about
that?

This last day is not an attempt to formulate a doctrine of hell. It
is more to use scripture to poke holes in the dogma that we've
been given, take a look at correct word translations and
meanings, and exercise some simple reason.   If I've learned
anything after reading several books and commentaries on hell,
it is not to be dogmatic. But I am hopeful, and am in very good
company with the likes of numerous Patristics, Hans Urs Von
Balthasar, Thomas Merton, and C.S. Lewis. I think it is ok to

be hopeful because God Himself is hopeful; the One who is not willing that any should perish and that salvation would come to all mankind.

Where to start? The first thing to understand is there are several different words for the one word *hell* we use in English. There is sheol, Gehenna, hades, and lake of fire. *Sheol* and hades are similar and are in reference to darkness or blindness. *Ha* is a negative and *eido* is to see; so hades literally means "to not see."* I would say a lot of people, including church folk, live a lot of their lives in hades, blinded by anger, bitterness, guilt, hatred, regret etc. If we can taste the kingdom of heaven on earth then we can also taste hell on earth. Gehenna was an actual place; a garbage dump outside of Jerusalem where trash was continually burned and dead corpses were placed in the time of war. A lot of references to Gehenna was a very real threat, such as Jerusalem being destroyed by the Romans in AD 70. The lake of fire we will get to later!

Whatever hell is, it is not separation from God! I will not re-hash how the incarnation of Christ, the God-Man, made our union with God an eternal reality but we will look at a few verses used to justify eternal separation. The parable of the rich ruler and Lazarus is often pointed at to indicate separation; a deep chasm between the ruler and Abraham. But what is causing this chasm? There is still communication between the ruler and Abraham, there is still relational language being used (my son...). It's the *attitude* of the ruler that is perpetuating the situation! He is still choosing to be stubborn concerning Lazarus, who he still sees as lower than him and expects to be served by him.**

David says in the Psalms 139:8, "even if I make my bed in Sheol (hell), there you are." How can we get away from God, He takes up all the space! In Revelation 14:10, even the devils are tormented *"in the presence of the holy angels and of the lamb."* The phrase, "weeping and gnashing of teeth" takes place in other portions of scripture where the religion of the Pharisees is being challenged by Jesus or Stephen indicating a state of hostility and holding on to a certain way of thinking. And how about IIThessalonians 1:9 NKJV? "These shall be punished with everlasting destruction *from* the presence of the Lord and from the glory of His power." The word "from" is *apo* which can be interpreted as the wrath, or passion, is coming *from* the presence of the Lord, and not necessarily that He is casting someone *away* from His presence.

So now that we cleared up that hell is not a separate location away from God, what the hell is hell? Did you ever think that hell is two different experiences of being in the presence of God? It says that God, who's very essence is love, is a consuming fire. Maybe God is the lake of Fire and Brimstone? Brimstone, *theion*, comes from *theios* which means *deity, divinity, godhead*. And the word *fire* in Revelation is the same Greek word *pur* as used in Hebrews 12:29 (God is a consuming *fire*). We have more of a view of fire taken from Dante's Inferno as retributive and torturous. But the view of fire in biblical times was not the same. It meant purifying, corrective, and restorative! It had an end goal in mind that was for our good (1Cor.3:15 NKJV: If anyone's work is burned, he will suffer loss; but he himself *will be saved*, yet so as *through fire*.). What if hell is the fiery passion of God's love that we can choose to resist and fight against? It's starting to seem to be more of a choosing on our part to strive and swim against the currents of eternal love. As C.S. Lewis said in *The Problem of Pain*, "hell is locked from the inside." Could someone conceivably resist God's love forever and ever? Maybe so, but eventually even death and hades are thrown into the lake of fire!

Lastly, since we value free choice so much in this world, could it be possible that we continue to choose in eternity? Why would we simply lose this personal freedom we cherish so deeply now in the next life? It's interesting that there is always an open invitation to drink from the waters of life freely. If we can continue to choose hell, the gates of the New Jerusalem still stay open day and night. It appears that we can also choose to walk through the Pearly Gates also; if we are willing to let go of whatever we are holding on to, put on our robe and ring, and join the party!

Is our will to self-destruct stronger than God's will to restore all things? Will God's purpose and hope for the destiny of the human race be thwarted by our own stubbornness? Scripture implies that at some point every knee will bow and every tongue will confess Jesus is Lord and even the valley of Gehenna is restored. Although there is so much mystery on this topic, I am more hopeful than I've ever been in my believing life and I hope you are as well!

The Mirror Study Bible by Francois Du Toit
**The Cosmos Reborn* by John Crowder

Part 2

CHAOS

Day 1 | Offering Our Breath

*"God has found a face in you that portrays him more
beautifully than the best theology. Your features, your touch,
the cadence of your voice, the compassion in your gaze, the lines
of your smile, the warmth of your person and presence
unveil him!"* Francois Du Toit

The human race has come a long way from what we believe to be
our first fruits that we should offer to God. Early religious cults
believed that they needed to sacrifice their first born child to the
gods as a first fruit offering. Yikes! But then we progressed to
offering the first fruits of our flocks through animal sacrifice
(yikes again!). Eventually it seemed like offering the firstfruits of
the harvest or crops is what God wanted. Today, most people
believe that our firstfruits are our time and money.

But if we think about what our first fruits actually are, it's the
very breath of God in your lungs; the very fact that you exist.
They are not *things* that you should *do* for God but the very fact
that you *are*. So if we want to honor God with our first fruits, we
really need to love ourselves and take care of our temples that
house the living God we serve. Our lives bring honor to Him

just like a work of art brings honor to its artist. Paul says that we are his workmanship, his *poiema*. You are His poem; He wants to write poetry with your life and express Himself through every detail of your smile, touch, and conversation!

You are a carrier of the living God Himself, who simply wants to *be* through you. God is not just a being and he is not all beings; He is beingness itself. He is life, love, vitality, creativity, and spontaneity. And your life is an expression of the Divine Life. We honor the Creator when we truly love ourselves, enjoy our own company, and are blessed by the communion of our own thoughts. We begin to be present; and the more we live in the present is the more we live in the Presence. We no longer future-trip about what tomorrow has to bring and neither do we focus on the mistakes and regrets of the past. We live in the eternal now. Every day becomes a gift, every interaction becomes sacred, and each moment is the opportunity for an encounter!

In western culture, we often validate ourselves through success, achievements, possession etc. Our identities seem to be completely wrapped up in these things. In other words, we live from the "I am not" tree and have to *do* in order to become something or somebody. But we truly honor God when we are most content and satisfied in Him and with ourselves. And when we love ourselves, it carries over into every facet of our lives. Our presence becomes contagious. We no longer *look* for blessings anymore; we *become* a blessing to others!

When we love ourselves we start projecting and radiating that love to every other person. Our cup becomes so full, it starts to overflow and we become a well that others can drink from. We become *poets* of the word; human expressions of the living God.

So offer God your first fruits. Breathe Him deeply into your lungs and exhale. The name of God YHWH is the sound of breathing. The holiest Name in the world, the Name of the Creator is the sound of your own breathing. These are the root letters of the Hebrew verb "to be." You are being sustained by The Name above all names. The Breath is sacred and it is life. Today, become aware of your breath. Breath in...and Breathe out... Say "God are you there?" Your breath is saying "I Am." You are in The Name and The Name is in you!

Day 2 | From Wilderness to Paradise

"You forgot the Rock who fathered you,
And forgot the God who gave you birth."
Deuteronomy 32:18

Do you ever feel like you're having a wilderness experience? You have no idea what got you there or where you are going. You seem to be circling around over and over to the same problems and struggles. Negativity has set in. Grumbling and complaining is your only communication. You've heard all of the promises of God but they don't seem to apply to you. Hopeless. Bitter. Why does this keep happening to me? How do I get out of here?

The Israelites had a wilderness experience that lasted forty years. They had left everything they knew in Egypt and were literally knocking on the door of the Promised Land. But something was preventing them from crossing the Jordan, into their destiny. There were giants on the other side. It says in Numbers "we were like grasshoppers *in our own sight,* and so we were in their sight." Did you see that? They *saw themselves* as grasshoppers. It was their own inferior mindset that was keeping them from paradise. They had forgotten who they were as the people of God and therefore they had forgotten where they were going. They were lost in the wilderness.

Moses was the prophet charged with the difficult task of leading the Hebrews out of the wilderness and into the Promised Land. How could he free them from their inferior grasshopper-mentality? How could he get through to a people that were so afraid, defeated, and hopeless; a people who wished they had never left Egypt and began to grow bitter towards God? It was at this moment that Moses started writing the Pentateuch, the first five books of the bible- "In the beginning....". He realized that they needed to look backward to move forward. "Remember! Remember your origin, who your Father is, and who you are! You have forgotten the Rock you were cut from and the God who danced with you!"*

We often hyperfocus on behavior when it comes to sin but the Greek word is *hamartia*; without form, without your full portion.** It is when we have a slip of the mind of who we are and we miss out on sonship. Interestingly, in the Old Testament the word for "without form" is *golum*, which is why JR Tolkien used the name Gollum in Lord of the Rings. The film occasionally flashes back to who Gollum really was; his true self, Smeagol. Sin isn't our lot in life. We are sons and daughters of the Most High. Jesus came to show us our face, as in a mirror. He is God's final word to us; a word of sonship. And Jesus is the Joshua figure who leads the people past the flaming sword into the promised land. Back into the divine dance.

Francois du Toit shares an ancient legend told by desert tribes in Morocco that records a unique story of the original fall. In the garden of Eden, the serpent told Eve that Adam had another lover hidden in a cave and therefore tried to convince her to eat a magical apple that would make her more beautiful. When Eve did not believe him, the serpent led her up a hill to the cave and told Eve to look inside. When Eve walked over to a water well in the cave, leaned over, and saw the reflection of a lovely woman, she didn't recognize it was herself and immediately took the apple and ate it. The legend concludes by saying that, whoever recognizes his or her reflection in the water can return to paradise!

*Francois du Toit- *God Believes in You*
**Francois du Toit- *The Mirror Study Bible*

Day 3 | Be-loved

"She loves. He is love. She is thirsty. He is a fountain."
Bernard of Clairvaux

The Song of Solomon is a conversation that takes place mainly between the Shepherd King and the Shulamite bride; a prophetic picture of Christ and His bride. I have also found that it is a very realistic portrayal of how most grow in their journey of understanding themselves and God. The verses below were chosen throughout the book to best summarize this journey. Because it is a conversation between multiple people, it is best understood by using a translation that distinguishes who is speaking (such as TPT used below).

The Shulamite: I know I am so unworthy, so in need
The Shepherd King: yet you are so lovely!
The Shulamite: I feel as dark and dry as the desert tents of the wandering nomads
The Shepherd King: yet you are so lovely--like the fine linen tapestry hanging in the Holy Place...though the curse of sin surrounds you, still you remain as pure as a lily.

Depending on what background we have or where we are in life when we first meet God, we often feel unworthy. We are more sin-conscious and focused on our own works while Jesus is persuading us of our beauty and purity based on His righteousness, gifted to us.

The Shulamite: my angry brothers quarreled with me and appointed me guardian of their ministry vineyards, yet I've not tended my vineyard within.

The Shepherd King: Promise me, brides-to-be, by the gentle gazelles and delicate deer, that you'll not disturb my love until she is ready to arise.

The Shulamite: until the day springs to life and the shifting shadows of fear disappear, turn around, my lover, and ascend to the holy mountains of separation without me.

A lot of our early journey is spent under someone else's vision; mostly an incorrect vision of how we must please God. We try to love the Lord with all our heart, soul, and strength. We also see ourselves as separated from God which causes us to "do" in order to close the distance. But the New Testament defines love as not based on our love for God but on His love for us. This really is the time to deeply drink of His unconditional love until something begins stirring deep within. "We love Him because

He *first* loved us" -1Jn4:19.

The Shepherd King: Your life has become clean and pure, like a lamb washed...Your lips are so lovely as Rahab's scarlet ribbon.

The Shulamite: I've made up my mind...in spite of shadows and fears, I will go to the mountaintop with you...yes I will be your bride. Make me your fruitful garden.

The Shepherd King: your life flows into mine...for you are my paradise garden!

As we start to contemplate the finished work of Christ, we begin to trust God and ourselves. Despite uncertainty and fear, we invite the Light into dark areas of our life and past for healing and restoration. It is here we start learning oneness; that God is in the most inward parts of us.

Shepherd King: Arise, my love. Open your heart, my darling, deeper still to me.

Shulamite: He is within me--I am his garden of delight. I have him fully and now he fully has me.

Shepherd King: Out of your innermost being is flowing the fullness of my Spirit.

Shulamite: I long to bring you to my innermost chamber—

this holy sanctuary you have formed within me.

Shepherd King: We will dance in the high place of the sky...Forever we shall be united as one!

At the end of the book, the back and forth dialogue between the Shulamite bride and Shepherd King converges into a synergistic duet. At this depth of union it can be difficult to determine where we end and God begins. He is so interior to us that we experience Him at the deepest levels of our personhood. Oneness.

Day 4 | The Recreation Story

"The renewal of creation has been wrought by the
Self-same Word who made it in the beginning."
St. Athanasius

The miraculous entry of the One foretold by the law and the prophets, who has split the time barrier in half, is something we need to pay attention to. Whether you look at the advent of Christ as one seamless sixth day creation or as a re-creation story, the bible is clear that the incarnation is indeed a creative act on behalf of God. With the birth of Jesus, the *Creator* has stepped into His *creation* to do some *creating*!

There are numerous parallels to draw between the creation account in Genesis and the Word becoming flesh in the Gospels. Genesis 1:1 reads, *"In the beginning* God created the heavens and the earth."* John begins his gospel account with a reference to Jesus; *"In the beginning* was the Word, and the Word was with God, and the Word was God."* Genesis 2:2 mentions, *"the Spirit of God was hovering over* the face of the waters."* This is mirrored in Luke 1:35 when the angel is disclosing the immaculate conception of the Lord to Mary the mother of Jesus; *"The Holy*

Spirit will come upon you, and the power of the Highest will *overshadow you."* And in the first creative act in Genesis, God declares, *"Let there be* light." In remarkably similar fashion, Mary replies to the good news, *"Let it be* according to your word."*

The similarities do not stop there. Throughout His ministry, Jesus performs multiple creative miracles such as giving sight to the blind by using the clay of the earth, healing and restoring limbs through the spoken word, and breathing life into Lazarus. It is of necessity that we recognize something here about the advent of the God-Man. Christ is the creator and sustainer of all life (Colossians 1:17). At the very moment you are reading this, you and every living thing are breathing Christological air. Everything was created by him and through him and nothing came into existence without him. In Him is the light of life. When he comes, all life comes with Him. Therefore, the life, death, resurrection, and ascension of Jesus had major implications for all humanity and for the entire cosmos.

The gospels aren't only a story about what happened to Jesus; they are a story about what happened to me and you as well as the whole creation. Everything proceeds from the Word and has always been in Him. Our lives did not begin with our earthly birth. God says through the prophet Jeremiah, *"Before* you were in your mother's womb, I knew you." (1:5) We were chosen in Him *before* the foundations of the earth. We didn't just jump into Christ to be co-crucified and co-resurrected with Him; we were in Him all along!

Born out of the virgin womb and raised out of the virgin tomb.* It says in Galatians 4:4 that Jesus was born of a woman, born under the law. He came in continuance with sinful humanity to discontinue and undo the fall. Everything of the old world, including the first Adam made from the dust of the earth, died at the cross of Christ. And then from the tomb that *no one had ever laid in before*, out of the dust of the grave emerges the Last Adam breathing a new world into existence!

Incarnation: The Person and Life of Christ by T.F. Torrance

Day 5 | Kingdom Consciousness

"The Kingdom of Heaven is really a
metaphor for a state of consciousness."
Cynthia Bourgeault

"Blessed are the pure in heart for they shall see God." Matthew 5:8 KJV. I used to look at this verse as if Jesus was saying, "Blessed are the morally good and upright for they shall see God." Maybe if one strives to be a moral and pure person, they will eventually see the living God and He will appear to them as an object. But is this what Jesus meant in this beatitude?

One of the most profound parts of Jesus's ministry is the forty days prior to His ascension. During this time, we see that He is not teaching his disciples *what* to see; He is teaching them *how* to see. As He prepares to depart from their sight, He is giving them a whole new vision of how to see, know, and interact with Him afterwards. To Mary at the tomb, He moves her away from physical sight and touch to a more interior way of engaging Him. *"Don't cling to me…"*.* The strangers on the road to Emmaus say to each other after walking with Jesus, "didn't *our hearts* burn…" as they are taught a knowing deep *within their* *hearts.* And then there is the interaction with Peter.

"Do you love me Peter? *Feed my sheep.*" This new way that is being taught of how to love and interact with God now is the most astounding. Jesus in effect is saying, "Peter, I know you love me. Now feed my sheep. Love me by loving your brothers and sisters and by taking care of them." Jesus is giving Peter an entire new foundation of how to engage and commune with the One he loves; by seeing God in all of humanity and ministering to Him there!

"Ripe are the consistent in heart; they shall see Sacred Unity everywhere."** Matthew 5:8. The Aramaic version of this verse gives a much clearer idea of what Jesus meant here. He is teaching how to see God: in all things and in all people. When one is ripe or ready to see in this single unitive way, they start seeing God everywhere. They don't see Him as an object, they see through the eyes of Christ; God becomes the seeing itself. They recognize that the Sacred Unity is all over and therefore they start seeing non-dualistically. Welcome to the Kingdom of Heaven!

It seems like the human race is stagnant right now because it is trapped in a deadlock of dualism. There are winners and losers, the first and the last, sacred and secular, black and white, red and blue, insiders and outsiders, those enlightened and those not etc. But not so in the Kingdom of Heaven. It is time for us to transcend dualism and bring the Kingdom of consciousness to humanity to co-create the new heaven and earth.

It seems like a big focus on the ministry of Jesus was attacking this dualistic way of thinking. His parables were not moral lessons but complete paradoxes that flipped the established mindset on its head. "You think that the last are bad but they actually will be the first, and the least are the greatest etc." He was introducing a Kingdom of consciousness; an entirely new way to see each other and to live in harmony and love together on the earth.

Blessed are the pure in heart for they shall see God. Those single eyed ones see and encounter God everywhere, every single day. They are the ones that take care of the least, feed the hungry, invite in the stranger, and visit the prisoner because they see the divine image in those people, and understand the Sacred Unity.

The Wisdom Jesus—Transforming Heart and Mind—a New Perspective on Christ and His Message by Cynthia Bourgeault
**Blessings of the Cosmos* by Dr. Neil Douglas Klotz

Day 6 | Ecstasy of Synergy

"As God comes out of Himself…in a 'departure from His own being' in his processions to create, sustain and save the world, so we are called to ecstasies, a departure from ourselves, as the act of our return to Him." Alexander Golitzin

One of the most frustrating challenges I had early in my spiritual walk was determining what God's will was for my life. I sincerely wanted to please God and earnestly desired to follow His will. But how was I supposed to be sure what God's will was for my life? How was I to know that it wasn't just my own will in *opposition* to God's will?

I used to view the will of God as something external from me; some specific path that had been determined by God that He wanted me to carry out. I constantly attempted to "seek" Him so as to find clarity on exactly what He wanted me to do. But I never heard any clear directions. I had strong intuition within me of what I was called to but I assumed this was just me and that it couldn't be trusted.

The story of Jesus praying in the garden of Gethsemane is one of my favorite events in His ministry. This is when Jesus is bearing the curse of sin by sweating literal drops of blood from His brow. I used to think that in this moment of weakness, Jesus was attempting to avoid the cross. "Let this cup pass from me." Is this really something that He wanted His disciples to witness?

When I speak of "will" I am referring to our deepest heart's desire and not the cheap unsatisfying fixes to these deep desires. The truth is that rooted within us, our wills are actually good and are made to flow in synergy with God's. Due to the fall, we had developed our own propensity to rationalize and reason our decision making based on our five senses. We began to live from the ego which only led to a desire for self-preservation and self interest. We basically became independent from God and from our truest self. So how do we make it back to what is most true within? "Let this cup pass from me, nevertheless not my will but yours be done." As I mentioned earlier, Jesus's entire life was a redeeming event and in this instance he was *redeeming our wills*!

We see in Gethsemane an astounding vicarious act on the part of Christ. He is not being schizophrenic between His own will and God's will. Jesus is stepping into our fallen humanity and taking our wills that had become independent from God and bending them back to their proper place of flow with God ("not *my* will but *yours* be done") Our wills are good and meant to flow in synergy with God's. We are co-laborers. This is what is truest about us and where we experience the most freedom. We are "created in Christ Jesus for good works, which God prepared beforehand that we should walk in them" (Eph. 2:10 NKJV).

According to early mystics, this co-laboring creates a mutual ecstasy. The divine will that God has for us lifts us up "out of ourselves" (*ekstasis*) to accomplish things that we could never dream of. At the same time, God's pouring of divinity into our humanity through incarnation pulls Him "out of Himself" putting Him in ecstasy! What makes you feel alive? What are the deepest yearnings within you? What gives you this ecstatic feeling? Trust that this is God's will for you, in you, and it will lead you down the right path!

*This chapter draws heavily from *Sons of Thunder Article-Christological Ecstasy* by John Crowder

Day 7 | Bride From His Side

"Behold the predestined plan of God:
Deity united with humanity."
John Crowder

Paul spoke often of the mystery that captivated his understanding. He said we have fellowship with the mystery; it may be something that we don't always fully understand but we are in union with this mystery. In other words, we can just let it disclose itself to us. Although it was hidden from all ages past, the mystery has been laid bare in the incarnation of Jesus Christ.

It was always the plan of God to take a bride. The whisper among the triune God was to share their overflowing fountain of love with creation and indeed was the very purpose for creation. The Trinity wanted to make something that they could bind themselves to eternally in consummated union. This was the plan all along. We see in Ephesians that this was God's doing, according to His will, His calling, His purpose, His choice, and His good pleasure.

I love how the Old Testament prophetically speaks on the Bride through people, events, and types. If Ephesians doesn't convince you of God's determinant will, maybe the story of Hosea will. As mentioned before, Israel was never chosen in exclusion of everyone else. They were called to be a light to the Gentiles; a sacrament to the wider scope of humanity. In the book of Hosea, God speaks to the prophet about taking the whore Gomer to be his wife. Again, this is directed to Israel but it is prophetically pointing to Christ taking his Bride. When God came in the flesh, humanity rejected, beat, and crucified Jesus and God used that very act to eternally bind himself to the human race.

Another astounding example is that of Adam and Eve. When Paul is teaching on the union of Adam and Eve from Genesis he says, "this is a great mystery" and compares it to the Church, the Bride. When Eve was created out of the side of Adam, the bible says he was put into a deep sleep. The actual word is *tardemah*, or trance. Adam was in ecstasy when his bride was created! When Jesus was suffering on the Cross during His passion, He was in ecstasy anticipating the coming of His Bride!* And out of His broken side the Church is created!

We are bone of his bone, and flesh of his flesh. Jesus is

continually convincing us of our value and worthiness in this marriage: "Every part of you is so beautiful, my darling. Perfect is your beauty, without flaw within. Now you are ready my bride, to come with me as we climb the highest peaks together" (Song of Songs 4:7-8 TPT). We think "but Jesus, you don't know what I did yesterday..." and he replies "You are lovely!" We say "but you don't understand my past..." to which he says, "You are lovely!" Jesus is not unequally yoked with His Bride!

Behold the mystery veil has been lifted! Awaken Bride to your purity and say yes!

Chosen for Paradise: The Inclusion of Humanity in the Saving Act of Christ by John Crowder

Day 8 | Oneness

"There is the free fall into the boundless abyss of God in which we all meet one another, beyond all distinctions, beyond all designations." James Finley

What does it mean to be a person? In the modern world we mostly associate personhood with rugged individualism and the uniqueness of one in separation from everyone else. In our society, to be autonomous and independent from the whole is what sets us apart from everyone else and is what is valued and pursued.

But the original evolution to the true meaning of the word "person" is much more astounding and beautiful. In the Hebrew bible, it started as a meaning for Israel's face to face (interface) communication with Yahweh. The Greek translation was *prosopon*, which literally came from the masks actors wore and indicated enlarged identities expressed through a megaphone. It meant the transference of personhood from one to another. Eventually the latin word *per sonare* was used to develop the doctrine of relationship within the Trinity and how they "sound through" each other*; the oneness and communion of the Whole would sound through each unique and distinct face of the Trinity. This was ultimately transferred over to psychology to refer to each individual manifestation of our shared humanity; what we now call unity with distinction.

It seems like the world and especially the church today is one or the other. Either we have unity without distinction, in which everyone in a body or group is completely the same and thinks alike. Or there is distinction without unity; a fragmented group of believers or people groups who only gravitate towards those most like themselves at the exclusion of those different. But we only experience true personhood when we have unity with distinction; when we come together and sound through each other. We are supposed to receive, in union with every person, their particular history, culture, and experiences and then allow it to sound through the face of our own unique face. This is what it means to be a person. We only truly know and find ourselves in relationships and through oneness with others.

The bottom line is we need each other. The word for compassion in the bible is *esplagchnisthe*; a very pregnant word (no pun intended). It means to literally carry one another in our bowels, like a mother carries a child as someone within her and as part of her. Wow! Can you imagine if we started having true compassion on each other, as Jesus was always moved with compassion for His fellow man? The healing of humanity would take place and the blinders would come off so we could see; deeper into each other and therefore deeper into ourselves.

Did you know we can also experience and encounter God in each other? We often think we only experience God as an individual Being. But He wants us to encounter him most in each other.

"When did we feed you, visit you etc.?" And Jesus replied, "When you've done it to the least of my brethren you have done it to me" (Matthew 25:40). He said you've done it *to* me, not *for* me. John writes, "God is love and *he who loves each other dwells in God.* But if you do not love your brother who *you can see,* how can you love God who you have not seen?" (1John 4). See where John is going with this?

When we lose ourselves in God and humanity is when we experience true mysticism. It is when we fall into the deep abyss of God to meet one another in transcendent oneness.

Eager to Love by Richard Rohr

Day 9 | The Unknown God

"Then will I know fully, even as I have been fully known."
I Cor. 13:12 Berea

A lot of believers often divide their lives into two parts; the life they had before they met God and the life after their conversion. Rather than seeing their life as a whole in which they become assimilated over time to spirituality, they tend to discredit their prior life as completely absent of God and insignificant. Is God really missing from the lives of unbelievers? Let's take a look at a summary of Peter Hiett's *Christmas in Athens* sermon for a quick history lesson surrounding Acts 17.

The Areopagus or Hill of Ares, was historically a rock outcrop that functioned as a court to resolve criminal cases and religious matters . In the 6th century B.C., a plague was ravaging the city of Athens causing immense suffering and death. The people were at a loss of how to stop the curse even after worshiping, to no avail, all of their known gods. In seeking the Pithian Oracle, they were told to find a man named Epimenides who would know what to do. When they found him in Crete and brought him to Athens, he suggested releasing several lambs to graze on the Areopagus in hope to find a God good enough to forgive their sins. Wherever a lamb laid down rather than grazed, they would mark the spot and sacrifice it to the unknown God. That very day the plague began to lift. They left one altar to this Unknown God in hopes that one day he would reveal himself and return as a friend of Athens; the One that had delivered them from the curse by the blood of a lamb.

Six hundred years later Paul "by chance" ended up in Athens after he was run out of Thessalonica and Berea. Upon debating with the pagan philosophers in Athens, he was brought by them to the Areopagus, now known as Mars Hill. Mars was the Roman god of war, which to a Jew like Paul, meant he was standing in the very heart of the Evil Empire. Paul began his discourse by using their altar to the Unknown God as a jumping off point. When sharing the gospel, one of the things he said was, "in God we live and move and have our being, even like your own poets have said." The poet he was "coincidentally" quoting was Epimenides, the man who had helped stop the plague 600 years ago! And now Paul was bringing the good news of Jesus, the slain lamb, as the Unknown God they had been waiting for!*

Paul says in this very same message (again, to pagans) that God is not far from any one of us and that we are His offspring. He was meeting the Athenians right where they were at to show how God had been operative in their lives and history. One of the great problems with evangelicalism has been the dismissiveness of the *shoes* people have walked in. Not only is it false to say God has been absent in their lives but it tends to communicate a dead-beat-father who has missed out on both the greatest joys and sufferings of His children. But He is, and always has been, present in our lives and to see that is incredibly healing!

Even in our doubt, confusion, and darkness, He is preparing altars in the hearts of every person, waiting to be revealed!

*Peter Hiett, *Christmas in Athens (Mars Hill Review, 1994), Premier Issue: 49-64.*

Day 10 | First Theophany of Moses

"Rejoicing and trembling at once, I who am straw partake of
fire, and, strange wonder! I am ineffably bedewed, like the
bush of old which burnt without being consumed."
Symeon the New Theologian

A theophany is a visible manifestation of God to humankind. Gregory of Nyssa considered Moses to be the patriarch of mystical ascent, demonstrated by three theophanies or encounters with God that Moses had; the burning bush, the dark cloud of unknowing, and seeing God face to face. We will use Gregory's three examples as a jumping off point for a deeper look into each theophany.

In Exodus Chapter 3, Moses walked up into Mt. Horeb, the mountain of God, to the sight of a bush burning with fire yet was not consumed. From the burning bush, God speaks and introduces Himself as "I Am who I Am." Here Moses sees the material saturated with divinity, the very fire of God burning within matter and yet it is not consumed! Understanding that Spirit *reveals* itself in matter, Moses has been initiated into the mystery of incarnation.

This example is clarified even more in the New Testament, as Jesus takes Peter, James, and John up into the mountain of transfiguration and shines through with the glorious Light of God for his disciples to see. Jesus is revealing the mystery of incarnation; that we too can burn with the fire of divinity and that we should let our lights shine before men as well!

Initiates of the mystery begin to see humanity in a whole new light. Like Moses, they *turn aside* to view all people as God-carriers and possess the ability to see beyond their mere human frailties and weaknesses. When Paul came to this realization, he said that he no longer looked at anyone "from a human point of view, according to worldly standards and values" (IICor.5:16 AMP). In other words, they begin to *re-spect* others: they look twice or deeper beyond the outward appearances of a person and are able to touch the essence within.

Day 11 | Second Theophany of Moses

"Emptied of all knowledge man is joined with the One who is altogether unknowable; and in knowing nothing, he knows in a manner that surpasses understanding." Pseudo Dionysius

"So the people stood afar off, but Moses drew near to the *thick darkness* where God was" (Exodus 20:21 NKJV). How is it possible to get to know the One who is described as never been seen, ineffable, beyond, above etc. Several people feel like the best way to get to know God is by knowing the bible would advocate for hours of daily prayer as the way. So it would appear that the best way to learn about God is through our own striving in prayer and bible reading?

The scribes and Pharisees of Jesus's time did both of these things better than anyone. They were extremely knowledgeable of the scriptures and probably spent hours in prayer each day. And the most fascinating thing is that Jesus boldly said to them, "none of you know God." Can you imagine the look on their faces? The most well respected religionists and examples of piety and understanding of the Divine were told that they had no idea who God was. When you think about what Jesus said, this is nothing short of astounding.

You see, you can never know God through religion. What we often do is limit the transcendent God to what we are able to learn about Him through our own perception and finite minds. The symbolism and metaphors we read in the bible give us a picture in our heads according to *our own* filter of these words. We gather information about God and consider this knowing God; and the more information the better. But God is not grasped by our own religious practices and humanistic understanding. When we create our own formulas and rituals, or adopt those of others, we can often trap God in our own dogma, frustrating how He wants to personally communicate with us. The more we approach Him with open hands, the more He discloses Himself to us by grace.

So who does know God best? Himself, of whom He has given us His fullness! Christ in us, the hope of Glory. The Spirit of Christ within us knows God for us and in us. We are smeared and saturated by the Holy One and need not that anyone teach us. The Knower, Jesus, has become known and now lives within. And now God wants to communicate and disclose Himself to us in the most intimate and interior way according to the deep uniqueness and distinctiveness of who we are!

One of the great paradoxes is that we learn most about God by unlearning. The forms and concepts we develop of God do serve an initial purpose and as Teresa of Avila described are the "living sparks" that draw us deeper into the mystery. But even the positive symbols and words we need to conceptualize God put Him in a box of our own finite understanding and need to be shattered over and over again by God, the Great Iconoclast. C.S. Lewis described this shattering as a mark of the presence of God.

This is why early thinkers such as Dionysius believed the best way to explain God is through negations, or what He is *not* (aka apophatic knowledge). This allows the mind to ascend higher beyond our own intellect, up through the cloud of unknowing, to where the Transcendent reveals Himself to us!

Day 12 | Third Theophany of Moses

"What we seek is what we are...you initially cannot see what you are looking for because what you are looking for is doing the looking. God is never an object to be found or possessed as we find other objects, but the One who shares your own deepest subjectivity—or your "self." Richard Rohr

When Moses asked to see the glory of God, God responded "You cannot see My face; for no man shall see Me, and live" (Exodus 33:20 NKJV). How is it possible that the Source of all being and the giver of abundant life can bring death to somebody? Also, didn't it say earlier in the same chapter that in the tent of meeting "the Lord spoke to Moses face to face, as a man speaks to a friend."? How do we explain this seeming contradiction?

If we take a closer look, the bible doesn't say that Moses will die; it says that he cannot see God's face *and live*! Moses had already been communicating with God *face to face* but this implied two things. For one, Moses was seeing God *face to face,* as an *object* outside of Himself. And secondly, He was merely *conceptualizing* God in his mind, *"as a friend."*

How can we drink from living waters within if we are seeking the Divine without? According to Richard Rohr in *The Immortal Diamond*, when we seek God as an object we can easily miss him because what we are looking for *is doing the looking*. We are looking for the X "up there" while we are standing right on it! In effect, God was telling Moses, "I'm going to show you a deeper and more experiential way of knowing me. As of yet, you have only known me as a mere human concept and outside of yourself. You are not truly living!"

It was at this point that God took Moses into the cleft or space of the rock. Moses had forgotten "the Rock he was cut from." He had forgotten his true origin in the Divine and that he came from the very breath and life of God! So God took him to his primordial beginning, the void, where there is nothing but limitless potential. He taught him how to live *from* God instead of face-to-face *with* God.

This is ultimately the life of holiness; to make space for God by sinking beyond the self. The Aramaic for holiness implies the extent to which we participate in the Sacred Oneness. *Qadash* means to create space to individuate and discover our unique place in the cosmic Unity. Sacred space allows us to expand and God to create within the expanse!

Day 13 | Sinking Into the Sacred Heart

"We join spokes together in a wheel, but it is
the center hole that makes the wagon move."
Lao Tzu

You may be asking yourself, "How do I actually live from the void? In practicality, what does living from the void even mean?" This profound lifestyle was best demonstrated by Jesus. He was able to live from the Source rather than his ego.

How was Jesus able to live from the bosom of the Father where he could boldly declare "I and the Father are one."? How was he able to do only what the Father was doing and say only what the Father was saying? There is a nugget of insight in the Bible when Jesus was asked by the rich young ruler, "Good Teacher, what must I do to inherit eternal life?" In his response, Jesus replied, "Why do you call me good? There is none good except God" (Luke 18:18-19).

Jesus did not live by *descriptions*, which is what our egos do. The ego creates all of these fractures within our personhood that we subconsciously live and act from and try to defend voraciously. Some of these fractures were developed from past experiences of trauma, rejection, and failure. Other fractures of the ego can even be "good" descriptions that we define ourselves with such as "spiritual people" or "teachers of wisdom." Jesus was able to sink into the heart of the Source, beyond ego and description.

Beatrice Bruteau in *Radical Optimism* gave some excellent examples of how this looks for us practically. If you can, imagine a circle with a dot in the center and all spokes extending out from the dot to the outer circle. The center dot is Christ; our own deepest reality or truest self. The spokes are the characteristics of Jesus; his wisdom, his love, his virtue etc. When we live subconsciously from our egos, we remain on the edge of the circle and rarely intersect with the spokes or characteristics of Jesus; the ego is too busy acting from and defending its descriptions. Awareness of these triggers allows them to no longer dictate our lives. Then as we sink into the center dot, into the deepest recesses of Christ, we begin to intersect with all of the spokes effortlessly. We don't need to *describe* ourselves as knowledgeable, because we don't *have* knowledge; we *participate* in knowledge! We no longer live but Christ lives in us!

Another example given by Bruteau is taken from the story of John leaning his head on the breast of Jesus during the last supper. Rather than imagining John doing this literally, picture Jesus sitting down and then John sitting down into him, with their faces gazing out from the same direction. John is now living from the bosom of Jesus, literally sinking into Him and living from the Sacred Heart!

Radical Optimism-Practical Spirituality in an Uncertain World by Beatrice Bruteau

Day 14 | Descent Mysticism

"I am one with the source insofar as I act as a source by making everything I have received flow again just like Jesus."
Raimon Panikkar

Today, I want to present you with an enticing invitation. Did you know that you are invited into the very mysticism of Jesus himself, the very experience that Christ had living in complete union from the bosom of the Father? In John chapter 1 Jesus is being followed by two disciples whom Jesus asks, "what do you want; what are you looking for? They in turn ask him, "Where do you dwell?"

Dwell is the Greek word *meno* and John uses it more than any other New Testament author. This is a word that is far beyond mere geographic location or a physical address for the house of Jesus. They were in effect asking Jesus, "where do you habitually dwell and live present in a place of seamless union?"* Jesus replies, "come and see for yourself." And he is saying to you, "come and see for yourself! Come and live from this place of seamless union from the heart of the Father." Astoundingly, according to John's estimate, we are already in this place by virtue of the incarnation!

This is not a place of preference. We cannot see people the way the Father sees people if we only want to see others the way we want to see them. We cannot say and do only what the Father does if we only want to say and do what we want to do. You can have great finished work theology and yet still live subconsciously from the ego. If we do not practice awareness, revelation is mere *information* until it is experienced, actualized, and embodied.

So how do we live from this interior place, from the vast mind of Christ? Paul maps it out clearly for us in Philippians Chapter 2: "let nothing be done out of selfish ambition or arrogance, let each recognize others more than themselves, don't only look out for yourself but look out for the interest of others as well. *Let this mind be in you* which was also in Christ Jesus, who being in the form of God, did not think it robbery to be equal with God but he made himself of no reputation and *emptied himself out.*"

This self emptying was referred to by the early church fathers as *kenosis*; the act of complete abandonment of Jesus to the divine will. And due to his humility, God exalted him and gave him a name above every other name! This is the path for us as well. We can't live ascended and seated with Christ in heavenly places while still trying to carry our ego's around. They don't go together. The way to ascend is to *descend* first; this is descent mysticism! When we pour out ourselves in humility then we will start seeing from our exalted position, from the vast mind of Christ!

* *The Mirror Study Bible* by Francois Du Toit

Day 15 | Born From the Beginning

"Jesus said: "if they say to you, 'Where do you come from?'
Say to them, 'We came from the light.'"
Gospel of Thomas 50

Today, we are going to be talking about one of the most well known biblical conversations that takes place in John 3 in which Jesus tells Nicodemus that he must be born again to see the kingdom. This verse has often been looked at in terms of salvation and something that takes place in the after life; "if you become born again then you will make it to heaven!" But remember, Jesus said to the Pharisees that the kingdom is within you; the Christ-life that is latent in each person and waiting to find full expression in their life. Jesus says that you must be born again in order to see the kingdom become operative in your life. So what does it mean to be born again?

The word *again* in Aramaic is *min d rish* which means from the beginning. In Greek *anouthen* also means from the beginning, from above, or the very first. What Jesus is doing is bringing us back to an origin far before our earthly birth; to an eternal beginning where we were always known! We come from the primordial beginning, the very life of God, which is why John says Jesus is the *light of life* that lights everyone coming into the world. In order to see the kingdom operative in our lives, we need to go back to the very beginning. Long before we were ever lost in Adam, and the sinful nature that we have come to identify so much with, we were found and formed in the image of Christ. Jewish mystics used to recreate this experience. By meditating on the very beginning, when the entire universe came into existence and spirit was first breathed into matter, they would see themselves coming out of the divine light and know who they really were. By saying we must be born by spirit and water, John is referencing this Genesis of the cosmos in relationship to us!

Jesus was stressing the importance for Nicodemus to go beyond his earthly origin and lineage in order to experience the kingdom. As stated before, Paul also came to this conclusion. Both Paul and Nicodemus needed to be separated from their earthly lineage and upbringing, which had become their entire identity, in order to see their divine origins. And we do too. So often the kingdom remains stagnant within us because our lives have become dictated by past traumas or false identities imposed upon us. Being born from the beginning *reboots the system* and allows us to identify with our true nature and Christ-likeness instead of the old man.

At this point, some may ask, "what about the born again experience I had?" I think a lot of us have had a radical, in space and time experience, including myself. So what is this? It is someone experiencing adoption. Again, adoption in Greek is not according to how we see it as being outside of the family, doing a transaction, and now we are inside of the family. It is coming into our full sonship, within the family we were always in, and being publicly disclosed as a son or daughter of the Most High! It is maturely living from our inheritance and the kingdom finding expression in our lives!

Jesus came to show us who we truly are and where we come from. Rather than identifying and therefore succumbing to a perpetual sinful existence, we see our original innocence in the face of Christ. Believing that we objectively come from the Primordial Light allows us to subjectively experience the kingdom in our lives. All things become new!

Day 16 | The Single Eye

"The eye through which I see God is the same eye through which God sees me. My eye and God's eye are one eye, one seeing, one knowing, one love." Meister Eckhart

In Matthew Chapter 6:22, Jesus said, "the light of the body is the eye; if therefore your eye is single, your whole body shall be full of light." This concept of the single eye is something the mystics looked into because it's such a profound revelation! So what does it mean for the eye to be single? Single in Greek is the word *haplous* which means to be folded together in undivided focus. Therefore, the way the single eye is mystically interpreted is to have your eye folded together with God's eye so you are both seeing through one eye!

How do we develop the single eye? We first need to see ourselves the way God sees us. We look through the eye of God into the very innards of ourselves and allow his light to flood our inner being with truth. All of our past experiences and disappointments, our traumas, rejection, insecurities, and failures are permeated with light and healing as we begin to perceive it all through God's love. As the body becomes filled with healing and wholeness, and the light completely submerges us we become flipped inside out and begin to see the world through God's eye! And as God simultaneously sees through your eye, the world becomes illuminated and beauty-full and we begin to see what He sees!

Once this happens, it is no longer us experiencing God "up there" or even somewhere "down here" within ourselves as an obscure "other." But the *seeing* becomes God itself, through one eye. In effect, you become a *mikrotheos*, a microcosm of Divine Reality. As a unitive one, God lives and experiences the world through you. You become a "thou" of the "I"; not just a part of God but a unique human expression of divine reality!

How do we know that we are on the right path? Well, how do you see yourself? Do you see yourself through the eyes of condemnation; as a broken, sinful person? Do you constantly beat yourself up for every mistake and are too critical of everything? Or do you see yourself in completeness, as God sees you, on a path of becoming your true self?

Secondly, how do you see others in the world? Are you seeing everyone through the eye of dualism? Do you see insider-outsider, us vs. them, first and last, winners and losers etc. Or

are you seeing the world through God's all embracing eye? Do
you see the Sacred Oneness everywhere? Blessed are these pure
in heart for they shall *see* God!

Day 17 | Mystical Knowing

"And while I stood there I saw more than I can tell and I understood more than I saw; for I was seeing in a sacred manner the shapes of all things in the spirit, and the shape of shapes as they must live together like one being."
Black Elk

I've found that the spiritual journey is one of becoming who we truly are. The deepest reality is that we are seated with Christ in heavenly places. But we don't always see, say, or do from this place. And this is ok, we need to have patience with ourselves.

The ego divides people into different camps and sees from a place of separation, fragmentation, woundedness, and self-preservation. When we see, say, and do from these places of the subconscious and allow it to direct our lives, we can become convinced that it is fate, as Carl Jung states, or even falsely identify with it as our true self in God. Religion can then turn into an extremely subtle place for us to hide from God and ourselves; the spiritual ego can become the last frontier for the false self to hide.

We often live by our own foggy perceptions and are directed by the "tree of knowledge"; the finite information that we have accumulated with our senses and then judge from. While the mind produces finite and limited knowing, the Spirit of Christ is infinite and produces a knowing of another order, beyond the five sense realm. While we often react to the illusions and emotions experienced by our normal senses, the Spirit perceives through a lens of love and *mishpat*, or God's "good judgment." Such truth buzzes with a frequency that we *first know* and recognize in our Spirit and then the mind *understands.*

This is mystical knowing directly from the mind of Christ, our true self and the One consciousness *behind* our thoughts. Our thoughts can be like tumultuous waves on a lake. We are not the waves but the person on the shore observing the waves. When we make this distinction the waves settle and the lake becomes still. We can begin to detach from harmful or non life giving thoughts and focus only on things that are true, noble, right, pure etc.

Initiates of the Mystery have had their third eye opened and can boldly say with Paul, "Have I not seen the Lord Jesus Christ?" They are seeing through the One unitive eye that recognizes God in everything and everyone; the entire cosmos is now perceived as reconciled into a harmonious whole. The Christ who has filled "all in all" challenges us to see God, the world, and each other in cosmotheandric unity. According to Raimon Panikkar, "the cosmotheandric intuition expresses the all embracing indissoluble union that constitutes all of Reality: the triple dimension of reality as a whole: the cosmic-divine-human. The cosmotheandric intuition is the undivided awareness of totality." What he proposes is to live so open to this triple dimension of reality, open to others, to the world, and to God that we might achieve harmonious communion with the all: the cosmotheandric reconciliation.*

*Raimon Panikkar, *Doctor Honoris Causa of the University of Girona, Prof. Josep-Maria Terricabras, 2008.*

Day 18 | Are You Ruling Over Time?

*"The Lord grants in a moment what may have
been unable to obtain in dozens of years."*
Philip Neri

In 2020 with the global pandemic, my work schedule changed. The work day started later and there was a lot more flexibility around when we had to be in. I remember how carefree those mornings were; if I was engaged in an interesting conversation with my wife or sharing a sacred moment with my children, I would continue to participate in the engagements and then leave when I was finished. There was little stress. As soon as the schedule changed back to normal with the start of 2021, I instantly felt pressure. The mornings became rushed and my blood pressure went up. I was under *chronos* again!

Do you rule over time or does time rule over you? *Chronos* is linear man-made time; we measure it with watches, seconds, minutes, hours etc. While it is important to be good stewards of our time, *chronos* can add unnecessary stress and pressure when it begins to rule over us. We make ever increasing lists of things to do with only so much time to get it done. We never seem to get ahead or break free of *chronos* and yet ironically, it sometimes can result in meager results and a lot of wheel-spinning.

But Paul tells us to make the most of time (*kairos*). *Kairos* is sacred time characterized by its non-linear and spontaneous occurrence. It is divinely inspired action at the perfect moment. When Jesus spoke of "goodness" and "blessedness", the Aramaic means *ripeness*; doing the right thing at the precise time.* *Kairos* creates new spaces *within* chronos; it brings eternity into the now. It is not time-less but time-full or time full-filled. When we aren't at the mercy of *chronos* but live within God's perfect timing, acceleration and extraordinary acts take place!

How can we open ourselves up to *kairos* moments? One of the best things is to live in the present. One of the biggest hindrances to tapping into *kairos* is by constantly living in the past or the future. Why do we do this so often? It's perfectly fine to have nostalgic moments about the past or get excited and plan for the future. But this is not what is always taking place. Often due to a lack of contentment in the present moment, we ruminate over how much better the past was or how much better the future will be. Because we conceptualize the past and the future in a snap-shot then we can freeze it still and then constantly compare it to the present. The ego loves to compare and differentiate!

When you live in a state of awareness, you will begin to notice divine appointments open up, timely conversations take place, and be taught profound messages through nature. Such things will propel us forward and expand our understanding far faster and deeper than the striving that takes place under *chronos*. And we also enjoy life more along the way!

Blessings of the Cosmos- Wisdom of the Heart from the Aramaic Jesus by Dr. Neil Douglas Klotz

Day 19 | Ascend to Transcend

"I will pour out my spirit on all people."
Joel 2:28 NIV

What does the empty tomb mean for humanity? How does the resurrection and ascension of Jesus Christ have practical implications for us beyond just faith? It seems like this has just become a historical event on the timeline of history; one that is important to believe in but may seem detached from everyday life and human interaction. If we move quickly beyond the gospel accounts surrounding the empty tomb, it is easy to miss some profound truths that can lead to a world community of harmonious love and belonging.

When Mary approached the tomb looking for the body of her Lord, she was confronted by two angels on each side. Richard Rohr describes this occurrence as a picture of the *ark of the covenant,* which had two seraphim on each side and carried the presence of Yahweh.* But in this case, the tomb/ark is empty; the *presence* is no longer there. So where did the presence go? We receive understanding by the appearance of Jesus and the conversation He has with Mary. He says, "do not cling to me, for I have not yet ascended to My Father; But go to My brethren and say to them, I am ascending to My Father *and your Father*, and to My God *and your God*." (John 20:17 NKJV)

Up until this point, Jesus had mostly been referring to God as "My Father." But now he is including me and you in that relationship. What Jesus was saying is that he was going to ascend to *transcend*. He was going to the Father to transcend and baptize humanity with His spirit of sonship and adoption. The ascension of Christ is so he could fill *all in all*. We see this in the gospel accounts as Jesus is seemingly appearing in different forms, transcending into a gardener, a stranger on the road to Emmaus, and a fisherman giving advice to the disciples.*

When Peter was attempting to explain what people were witnessing on Pentecost, he related Jesus' ascension to the right hand of God with the shedding forth of the spirit on *all flesh*. Now we are the body of Christ in the world. We often repeat the statement of Jesus that "we would do greater things than him" as something that each individual will accomplish on their own. But if you look at the context of the statement, he finishes it with "because I go to my Father." Because Jesus has ascended to transcend, the universal body of Christ all over the world has accomplished more and greater works than the one man Jesus. "It is better that I go so that I can send the Spirit."

II Corinthians 5:17 KJV declares, 'if any man be in Christ, he is a new creature: old things are passed away; behold, all things are become new." We have looked at this as a conditional statement that only takes place in certain individuals at the moment of conversion. But it is not a condition. *Therefore* is how the verse starts off. It is a conclusion based on an earlier verse: "the love of Christ compels us, because we judge thus: that if One died for *all*, then *all* died." All have died and now all are new creatures!

The word creation *kainos* implies that we are something altogether new, and also part of a whole new world. All died with Jesus; the entire cosmos was baptized in His death and now we are grafted into a new heaven and earth as a *kainos* reality! The church was never to exist in exclusion from everyone else. It was supposed to be a living sacrament or signpost that births Christ realities to which everyone has been made part of!

* *The Universal Christ* by Richard Rohr

Day 20 | Another Ordinary Miracle Today

"There are only two ways to live your life. One is as though nothing is a miracle. The other is as though everything is a miracle." Albert Einstein

A miracle is a surprising and welcome event considered to be the work of a divine agency. Everyone loves miracles; especially those who have a stronger belief in the supernatural. Some even will spend much time and money pursuing miracles through spiritual practices or by attending conferences; possibly listening to specific teachers who focus on this topic. Maybe they see miracles once a week? Once a month? Every new conference? But what if we could see miracles every day, all of the time?

Sometimes a lot of people live from teaching to teaching, conference to conference, and encounter to encounter. To them, these are the only sacred moments of the supernatural, when God miraculously intervenes and they receive a "touch" from God. The reason for this, is seeing God as *above* history; that the supernatural is separate from the natural and occasionally God comes down from heaven to do something magical. But we truly start seeing miracles everywhere when we understand God as being *under* history; that He is and always has been present in human history and in our own lives! Sometimes it is simply more evident than others.

Do you want to experience the encounter of a lifetime or live a lifetime of encounter? We can experience miracles every day if we have eyes to see. Spirit and matter are woven together and we encounter spirit within matter. God is everywhere and in everything. When we start truly believing this, the veil between heaven and earth becomes thin. Every second is an opportunity for encounter. Each conversation becomes meaningful. All of nature starts blazing with divine glory. It's like we are seeing in a whole new dimension and the natural has transcended into the supernatural. Every moment is sacred. The sleeping infant on our chest. The deep communion of two friends confiding in each other. The parent staying up sleepless for nights tending to a sick child. The last moments spent with a loved one as they breathe their last breath. Awareness of this causes us to see with new eyes. Nothing is a coincidence anymore and every thing that once seemed mundane is a work of divine agency; a miracle.

It is amazing to me that out of all the things Paul could have talked about such as his heavenly raptures, the many healings he witnessed, the miracles he performed etc., his major focus was on Christ in himself and in everyone else. In fact, he didn't mention one miracle performed by Jesus! What captivated his understanding was the Cosmic Christ. Paul was completely out of his mind realizing that Christ was everywhere. Not one person was a mere mortal any longer. The divine had penetrated everything!

"Once we know that the entire physical world around us, all of creation, is both the hiding place and revelation place for God, this world becomes home, safe, enchanted, offering grace to any who look deeply."- Richard Rohr*

*Richard Rohr, *The Universal Christ (Center for Action and Contemplation, 2019), 6-7.*

Day 21 | The Keynosis to Life

"Seek ye first the kingdom of God and his righteousness
and all these things will be added to you."
Matthew 6:33

We are going to take a look at the above scripture in Aramaic, which is the original language that was spoken by Jesus. Aramaic is such a beautiful language that is equally deep and rich. It is also loaded with meaning, a lot of which gets lost when translated to a limited language such as English. In the context of this verse, Jesus is basically telling us to stop worrying about everything. Maybe as you read this, you are going through something that is making you anxious?

There is a well-known quote by Richard Rohr that states, "God often comes to you disguised as your life." If we allow it to, the world can be a mirror that teaches us. Each person that comes into our life, every opportunity that we have, and all circumstances can teach us deeply about ourselves and about God. So how are we responding to people we deem difficult? What do we do when a challenging financial circumstance comes up? Do we continually point the finger at things external to us as the problem or do our minds spin into worry, fear, and despair?

So within the context of the worries of life, let's get back to the verse, starting with *seek ye first*. Dr. Klotz elaborates on the Aramaic beautifully. The word for first is *luqedam*; the first, as in the primordial origin of the universe. Jesus was directing us to seek this alpha point to show us that we are connected to something bigger than our small self. We are one with the cosmos.

What are the *things* Jesus is talking about in the above verse? The Aramaic for things is *kulhyen halneyn*. This is not only referring to material things but all things, emotional and mental states, and the never ending day to day concerns we experience. And lastly *shall be added unto you*. Added is *mithausepheyn* which contains a middle eastern root meaning "to prostrate the sense of small self in order to receive the self of the One."*

In putting this all together, Jesus is encouraging us to stop separating ourselves from God, from the One who we are in seamless union with! This is what the ego does; it tries to independently seek things and solve problems from a place of worry and self-striving. When we react to life's problems in this manner, then we detach ourselves from the One that we are fastened to. On the contrary, when we pour ourselves into the universe, God *through the universe* pours back into us. We are in a divine dance with God and we have a law of reciprocity with the cosmos. As we live in awareness of our place in the Uni-verse, God will provide for us! The "things" start to attach themselves to us!

*All Aramaic translations taken from *The Hidden Gospel: Decoding the Spiritual Message of the Aramaic Jesus* by Dr. Neil Douglas-Klotz

Day 22 | The Undoing of Adam

"What has not worked for me has taught me the depth of who I am. The broken parts of my past are not monuments made in stone, but doorways through which I passed into a better tomorrow."
Steven Charleston

Too often we trudge through life carrying the painful memories of our broken pasts as well as the paralyzing guilt from the poor decisions we have made. In many cases, our pasts can program the subconscious to where we automatically respond a certain way from these areas of pain. This can lead to feelings of inadequacy and a constant blaming of our present reality on external circumstances and other people (or God). None of us escape the human condition so we can all testify, to varying degrees, of past hurts and failures. But our lives don't need to be directed by such things.

I want you to imagine a long rope to represent your life from birth to present. Along the way we develop a lot of knots in the rope from past experiences and traumas. Those knots can hinder the flow of life from the Source and make it unable to find full expression in the present moment. Instead, rather, we respond to people and situations from these "knots" and our perception of reality becomes skewed. So how can we undo these knots and live from the Life?

It is an essential starting point to first gaze at Jesus for our objective reality. Adam has been undone. The life of Jesus was a blow by blow destruction of the Adamic man until He fully restored our original innocence back to us in the garden. As we said earlier, the gospel writers corresponded the birth of Jesus with the *creation account* in Genesis. Then Jesus comes back *through the desert* to overcome temptation in the wilderness. Later on, we find Him *back in the garden* (Gethsemane) in which man first ran away from God (just like the disciples ran away from Jesus). And finally Jesus follows the rabbit trail all the way back to *the Tree*, outside of the city, where on the Cross He looks steadfastly into the face of God during his greatest trial and refuses to lose faith. And now after burial and resurrection, Jesus walks from the dust of the grave as the second Adam in the garden (Mary confuses him for a gardener!). All things have become new!

This is our reality; we have been co crucified and raised with Christ anew. Sometimes though, we may still find ourselves subconsciously identifying with the past and allowing it to keep us from healthy relationships and/or stepping boldly into our destiny. This is why being born from above is so important (going back to the beginning). Seeing the Light of Life that we come from allows us to untangle the knots in the rope. We can stop identifying with our failures and rejection that have run our lives for so long and begin to identify with the true self.

I am not saying to be completely dismissive of the past, which can lead to its own set of problems through suppression and denial. Some of these "knots" need healing and for broken memories to be restored. Jesus can do that as well. You don't need to beat yourself up about the past, it can lead you to a better tomorrow!

Day 23 | Becoming Prayer

"All your living is prayer in my eyes."
Julian of Norwich

All sincere Christians earnestly desire to be pleasing to God. They initially go about this by reading the bible and especially through prayer. Prayer is the communication line between us and God and as such is a praiseworthy endeavor. It is something that we do, often alone in a quiet place. But as we advance on the spiritual path, prayer is no longer something that we do; we become prayer! How else are we to fulfill Paul's exhortation to pray without ceasing?

The mystical way is a journey to the very center of ourselves, where we find God. We are one-ed with Him. Something quite astonishing takes place as we meditate on this mystery; we wake up inside Christ's body. Symeon the New Theologian described this as light illuminating every last and hidden part of our body, even what we considered damaged and shameful. We are transformed from the inside out and realized in joy as Him!

Having this awakening take place changes the way we view life.

We start to recognize God at the very tip of everything we do, even the most mundane things. Pierre Telhard de Chardin, in *The Divine Milieu*, captures this realization perfectly: "He (God) awaits us at every instant in our action, in the work of the moment. There is a sense in which he is at the tip of my pen, my spade, my brush, my needle–of my heart and of my thought" (Harper Perennial, 28). We start seeing our very lives as an offering to God, a sweet savor. Prayer is no longer something that we *do* because it has become who we *are*.

Dame Julian says of God, "in Himself He is Existence itself." Our lives become one of being, a life well pleasing to God. And as we see God smile upon us we start to smile upon ourselves and simply enjoy our own company. Everything is an offering and prayer to God no matter how small. Like Brother Lawrence said, "I turn my little omelet in the pan for the love of God." We now are praying without ceasing.

When Teresa of Avila was asked what she did in prayer, she responded "I just allow myself to be loved." This is the prayer life that is most pleasing to God; the perpetual receiving of His love and the enjoyment of a life well lived in confidence of that love

Day 24 | Mutual Indwelling

"We are held together like stars in the firmament with ties inseparable. These ties cannot be seen, but we can feel them. We are all one." Nikola Tesla

In reference to how we should interact biblically with our fellow man, it is often said to "love your neighbor as yourself, and if you don't love yourself then you can't love your neighbor." This is true to some degree but what is implied by this explanation is that you should love others like you love yourself. However, that is not what the verse says upon closer look. It is saying in effect that you should love your neighbor *as* yourself; as an *extension* of yourself!

We are all one, mutually indwelling one another. It is the ego that creates the illusion of separation from everyone. When we live life superficially from this illusion, we end up only looking out for ourselves and we lose sight of the oneness we share with humanity. As we sink into the deeper recesses of our center we enter the One, intersecting the many, and experience communion from within others.

When you carry people in your heart and are willing to enter in their heart, you often experience the indwelling. Have you ever started thinking about a friend and the next moment they call you? Or feel deep sorrow for someone close only to find out they are going through a crisis and feeling that same sorrow? This also happens with people we are not as close to. We have a dream about someone we knew 20 years ago only to hear from them the next day. This is not coincidence; you are experiencing oneness.

We are designed for community with each other. But often we feel like we are in a zero sum game with our fellow brothers and sisters. You don't need to see a person's gain as your loss or their victories as your failures. This is looking at things from a position of lack. When we live from a mindset of abundance due to our mutual connection in the One, your victory becomes my victory, your win my win, your loss my loss. As the human race, we all win together or we all lose together. Waking up to this reality allows us to see our true selfhood in communion with the Whole.*

Beatrice Bruteau writes that we could even experience communion with the Saints, both past and present, in this abiding. She mentions in *Radical Optimism*, "these people are mystically present to us in the holy communion of saints; the deep reaches of our consciousness indwells theirs and theirs, ours; at their level they come available to us."* Truly, the deeper we go the more united we become!

*Beatrice Bruteau, *Radical Optimism-Practical Spirituality in an Uncertain World (Sentient Publications, 1993, 2002), 139.*

Day 25 | Other Old Testaments

"The gospel dignifies every culture as a
valid vehicle for God's revelation."
Richard Twiss

We initially imagine God as having a very limited role in the ancient cultures and histories of the world. It seems as if He was only present to the Jews while every other people group was in pure darkness. But as we progress on the spiritual path our vision of God should be getting bigger, not smaller. We realize that Christ was present in creation from the beginning of time, then incarnated in the person of Jesus, and now resides in all. We also begin to see that there were numerous "old testaments": God preparing other cultures in unique ways for the revelation of Jesus Christ at his advent.

Most ancient cultures read the "first bible", creation. Paul says in Romans 1:20 NIV, "For since creation of the world God's invisible qualities–his eternal power and divine nature–have been clearly seen, being understood from *what has been made.*" The Native Americans had a great reverence for the earth and there was a prevalent belief in a monotheistic creator who self-revealed in creation. Steven Charleston, a Christian bishop and Choctaw identified several parallels to Israel and his people; they believed they were a chosen people in covenant with Creator. They had an ancestral migration story to a sacred land that was promised to them by virtue of that covenant and also collected their memories using a variety of literary methods (like a testament). Charleston also states that his people eventually came to look for a messiah who would lead them into the next chapter of their sacred history.*

The early Greeks were another culture who had their own "old testament." The Church fathers recognized in these pre-christian Greek philosophers an unfolding of wisdom through foreshadowings and glimpses in preparation for the revelation of Christ. They believed in one God, the uncreated Cause of the universe. The Greeks talked about the *Logos* as being the pattern of the world and the first principle of existence and sustenance for the creative process; and that one should live according to this Logos. The apostle John saw no problem in using this same word to describe the Christ. Also, *mysterion* (mystery) and metamorphosis (transformation) were terms frequently used by Paul that had long been associated with Greek religion and philosophy.** On Mars Hill, Paul also quoted ancient Greek poets as a source of revelation when contextualizing the gospel for the pagans.

In the *Tao Te Ching*, Lao Tzu writes about something similar to the Logos called the Tao or the Way. He had a revelation of the primordial Source that existed before heaven and earth and sustained and encircled everything. The Tao was infinitely humble and humans should live in flow and harmony with the Way. Lao Tzu had several teachings that were very similar to the teachings of Jesus, such as the life of self-emptying and he even alluded to the Trinity.**

These are only three of the numerous cultures who had their own old testaments to lead them into understanding the person of Christ. God has not been absent among His children; He has progressively provided light to point them to the Light. Knowing the Logos has always been in each person allows us to honor the wisdom of all cultures and traditions; and to see that all mystics speak the same language.

* *The Four Vision Quests of Jesus* by Steven Charleston
** *Christ the Eternal Tao* by Hieromonk Damascene

Day 26 | Love's Logic

"This trinitarian relationship, this abounding and joyous communion, this unspeakable oneness of love, is the very womb of the universe and of humanity within it."

C. Baxter Kruger

You didn't begin in your mother's womb. You began with a whisper deep within the very heart of the eternal God. This conversation started from before time and indeed is the very logic (logos) and purpose of creation. The apostles James, John, Peter, and Paul all saw it. It made all the difference in their lives and ministries and it will in yours too. You were made to be a part of something. You were made to participate in the dance. You were made for infinite love.

The Trinity had a passionate unquenching desire to share everything they had within themselves with humanity. Out of their abundance and overflow of selfless perfect love, they determined to create something that they could eternally bind themselves to in consummated union. It couldn't be any other way because this is the very nature of who God is. His fountain of love is full and he wants to lavish it on everybody and everything. Behold, the eternal plan of God! He always intended on being God with us!

On the eve of creation, the Alpha and Omega in one divine glance saw from beginning to end and made preparation. The lamb was slain from before the foundations of the earth. We were found long before we were ever lost. To be more precise, we were chosen in Christ before there was any such thing as a fall. God was never taken off guard by what happened in the garden. Like a slowly budding flower, there has never been a moment that this world has been kingdomless. It is all one seamless thought. Many early church fathers saw all of human history as salvation history. From the very beginning, the Word was on its way to become flesh in the incarnation; the Word of God spoken from eternity and made manifest in Jesus.

Some of us believe that the earth was created *ex nihilo* or out of nothing. Jewish mystics thought the opposite; it was more like nothing out of something! They referred to God in the beginning as Ein Sof, unending or infinite. The idea of Ein Sof is that God who is eternal and infinite "Something" withdrew a space within the very center of His being and made a void to create within. Then, from His very breath and life began filling the void with

Spirit and matter.* There has never been a separation of spirit and matter from God's perspective; this is something we picked up from Greek Western thought.

We come from eternal seed, the very *ruach* or breath of God. And we have always been associated with Christ, the alpha and omega. The moment creation burst forth from him is the moment it began being drawn back to him. The beginning is the end and the end is the beginning. All things begin and end in Christ.

*_The History of Time_ by Peter Hiett

Day 27 | More Revelation Already!

"Revelation is always already; it entails a sense of deja vu."
Daniel Matt

How do we get more revelation from God? This is often a sincere question asked from those searching for enlightenment. But it isn't so much a matter of revelation; God is always revealing. It is more a question of reflection. What are you reflecting?

It says in Ezekiel 1:1 NKJV, "as I was among the captives by the River Chebar, the heavens were opened and I saw visions of God." Jewish mystics looked to the prophet Ezekiel as the authority on revelation. They often associated gazing into the water as a meditative technique. *Chebar* in Hebrew means already, so to reword the verse, "as I was among the captives by the river already...I saw visions of God." So to paint a picture imagine Ezekiel gazing into the river waters, deep in meditation. A vision of God appears above him but Ezekiel sees it in the water first, and then turns to look at the vision. This is what revelation feels like; almost like a sense of deja-vu. We are seeing something new yet simultaneously we knew it already; almost like a primordial remembering!*

God is always revealing but what are you reflecting? Jewish mystics saw reflected in water the highest deepest dimension of self (It is interesting that humans are mostly made up of water!). So how do we reflect what God is revealing? The biggest hindrance to reflection is the tumultuous waves of the ego. When a person's life is dictated by this subconscious program, it matters little what is being revealed to them. It ends up being filtered through lenses of hurt, preservation, and self-interest. The pure revelation that God is communicating ends up being obscured by the desire for attention and self-promotion. Only still waters will reflect the undiluted revelation. The waters can be calmed through awareness, honesty, light, and truth.

Divine revelation always bears fruit in relationship with its origin. The tell-tale sign of a true vision is a transformed life. Still the waters within and reflect what God is revealing!

The Essential Kabbalah by Daniel Matt

Day 28 | A Tale of Two Trees

"On either side of the river was the tree of life, bearing twelve kinds of fruit, yielding its fruit every month; and the leaves of the tree were for the healing of the nations. There will no longer be any curse." Revelation 22:2-3

Cain and Abel were brothers. Because God respected the sacrifice of his brother but not his own, Cain grew jealous of Abel. Then one day, as the brothers conversed in a field, Cain's jealousy possessed him and he murdered Abel. This is the first murder recorded in the Bible.

At first glance it appears that God favored Abel more than Cain. But there is much more going on here indicated by the sacrifices that each brother brought to the Lord. Abel was a keeper of sheep and brought the firstling of his flock to the Lord. But Cain was a tiller of the ground and brought the fruit of the ground as an offering to God. Why did God accept Abel's and not Cain's?

The sacrificial system didn't start with Moses. After Adam and Eve fell in the garden, God made skins for them. It's implied that an animal was sacrificed and blood was shed in order to cover the shame of Adam and Eve. On the other hand, tilling the ground by the sweat of your brow was associated with toiling under the curse. The former represented a righteousness *by faith* as a free gift provided by God while the latter was an attempt to be independent and strive to produce one's *own righteousness*. Abel saw that righteousness was not something that could be earned but only through faith in the righteousness of the One. Cain was still operating under the curse trusting in the fruit of his own labor to produce righteousness.

Really this is the tale of two trees. The tree of life represents a life of dependence on God; a life sustained by communion, intimacy, and receiving of His fullness. A life that completely trusts in the faithfulness of God to grace us with righteousness and holiness. The tree of life is the tree that Jesus hung on and where the divine exchange took place. The other tree is the do-it-yourself tree. This represents a life of lack where one has to strive and toil in order to become spiritual. It is the tree of the knowledge of good and evil. The word for evil is *poneros*, which means a life of hardship and annoyances and labor.* This is the tree that Cain lived from and where most people still live from today.

Another interesting point to ponder; maybe Cain and Abel represent two sides of each one of us? Abel is *Hehbel* in Hebrew, which means breath and *Cain* means to possess. Abel is a state of *being* while Cain represents *doing* to acquire. Breath in the Bible is closely related to spirit. When Cain killed Abel he cut off the divine breath and spirit became silenced in matter. This is what our ego's do. The false self tries to silence the divine spark in us and becomes the reigning entity in our lives, suppressing the true self from emerging...until we awaken!

The new heaven and the new earth speak of a tree in the middle of the new Jerusalem whose leaves are for the healing of the nations. But when our eyes are opened we partake of this tree now as a divine be-ing!

The Mirror Study Bible by Francois Du Toit

Day 29 | The Holy Presence

"The Word is living, being, spirit, all
verdant greening, all creativity."
Hildegard of Bingen

The Spirit is pure spontaneity, creativity, and vibrancy, which is why I've found most books and teachings on the subject unhelpful. The Spirit is too much of an enigma to fully explain it with individual experiences, concrete formulas, and dogmatic principles. I will not attempt to showcase a new formula but simply to share some scriptural conclusions that I've arrived at which can give the reader incredible peace and freedom.

First off, who "has" the spirit and how do you "receive" it? The English text in most bible translations seems to make this into something that some have and others do not, or only until they get it transactionally. But if we look at the Greek, we see this is not the case. When Paul says in Romans 8, "those who *have* not the Spirit", the Greek for "have" is *echo* which is exactly where we get the English from. What Paul is saying is that the Spirit is not resonating with some, or echoing. Similarly in the case of the word "receive", people are not getting something they don't have.

The Greek word is *lambano*, which means they are not identifying with the Spirit.* It says through the prophet Joel and repeated by Peter on pentecost that the Spirit has been shed forth on *all flesh*. Some are just not identifying with it.

Secondly, what does the Spirit do? The Spirit testifies of Jesus and always points toward Him and His finished work (John 15:26). The Spirit does not condemn us! A Lot of people condemn themselves and say that the Spirit is "convicting" them. There certainly comes an initial sorrow where we are confronted with choices that aren't working for us, and it is good to follow our conscience and not defile it, but the Spirit actually convicts us of our *righteousness*! (John. 16:10). When addressing His believers He plainly states what the Spirit is convicting us of!

Thirdly, we have the Spirit in Person, not in portion. The Trinity travels in a 3-in-1 package. It seems like we have separated the Person of the Spirit from the Trinity as a mere force that we can wield, get more of through spiritual disciplines, or lose through wrong behavior. We are certainly more sensitive to the Spirit at times depending on where we are in life but the Spirit is not coming and going in measures. Again, it is a Person who we have fully and we can allow to fully have us!

Even the baptism of the Spirit is not an inpouring from heaven but an outpouring or flooding of our senses from the living waters within! The word for baptism is *baptizmo*, which means dunking. When we experience this, the inner Spirit floods or immerses our outward natural senses. When does this happen to us? When Peter is explaining the Pentecost experience to onlookers, he says that because Jesus is "exalted and seated at the right hand of God" is why it is happening. In other words, it has already happened! Believing will allow you to experience it in your own unique way!

Lastly, how do we "hear" from the Spirit? (hear is in quotations so as not to limit the many ways God speaks; knowing, feeling, through others, circumstances, life etc.) I believe this one trips up people most. Countless books have been written about this, all with different methods. Is it the still small voice you hear in silent contemplation or the thunderous imprint you feel in your spirit? Honestly it might be one or the other, both, or neither. It may be one way today and another tomorrow.

What I've found is that God is so personal to us and the Spirit communicates to us in distinct ways that are unique to who we we are. Although someone else's method might be right in line

with who we are, attempting others' formulas usually can frustrate grace and how the Spirit wants to communicate personally with you. If you are struggling to be still, try doing some chores, or walking contemplatively. As we grow in self-awareness as well as just simply opening our hands and heart to the spontaneity of the Spirit, we will begin trusting our intuitions and "hear" constantly!

To bring this all together, the Spirit is something fully on the inside of us and not something that we have to manipulate from beyond. Just as the Spirit led Jesus into the wilderness, it will prepare us for our own vision quest through the wilderness of our psyche to bring about self-realization and discovery.

* *The Mirror Study Bible* by Francois Du Toit

Day 30 | Co-Creators

"The power of the stars is nothing compared to the energy
of a person whose will has been freed...and who is thus enabled to
co-create the cosmos together with God." Thomas Keating

One of my favorite sayings of Francois du Toit is "the bible is not a behavior manual, it is a book about Immanuel!" God with us. So many people think that the ultimate destiny of the Word was to end up in the bible. But the Word became flesh and God is about incarnation. When someone creates a majestic musical piece, it isn't supposed to be put on a stand and stared at. The notes are meant to be audibly expressed and to echo throughout the ages.* So our lives are meant to be living epistles, studied and read by all!

In II Peter 1:5, we are told "giving all diligence, add to your faith virtue, to virtue knowledge, to knowledge self control" etc. It ends up mentioning eight different characteristics that seemingly lie external from us. At best, this is something that we can ask God to add to us in prayer and at worst, we can try and work to produce these things on our own. But the verse actually begins with "for this reason" or "therefore". Well, what is the "therefore" there for?

At the beginning of the chapter, it says that Jesus has made us partakers of the divine nature and given us all things that pertain to life and godliness. So when did this happen? More specifically, how does God give gifts? There is a verse in Romans that says when Jesus ascended on high he gave gifts to man. So we often think that God is still sending down spiritual gifts from heaven. But this is actually taken from Psalm 68 which says, "you have ascended on high and *received gifts* among men." Every gift that God gives has already been received into our humanity. By virtue of the incarnation, God becoming human, He has made us partakers of His divinity. Everything that we need is already on the inside of us!

Then why does Peter tell us to give all diligence to "add" these characteristics to ourselves? The word "add" in English is a much longer, and more meaningful, word in the Greek called *epichorigeo*. It is actually a three part word but to simplify, we almost see the word chorus on the inside and the word carries the meaning of a chorus or choir conductor! So what Peter is telling us is to become acquainted, by faith, with these characteristics that are already on the inside of us. Like a music composer, we start creating a musical symphony with our lives and become a living masterpiece from the inside out!*

The interesting thing about this Chapter is the word *epichorigeo* is used later on; except this time, Jesus the Great Conductor is leading us into this symphony!* Everyone is a co-creator with God which is why it is so important what we believe about ourselves. We are powerful beings made in the image of God. When we live from the inside out and speak words into the atmosphere we create our reality. This is why Jesus is always pointing to our wholeness and completeness. We become energized when we acknowledge every good thing that is in us; in Christ! He wants us to co-create with us in our personal worlds as well as make a whole new world with Him!

*_The Mirror Study Bible_ by Francois Du Toit

"The path of mysticism is a journey into the very core of your being…where you find God."

spoken logos

Connect with Brett Derrico

Email: spokenlogos7@gmail.com

Instagram: @spoken_logos

Made in the USA
Middletown, DE
27 October 2023

41370025R00108